GW00863418

500 HEALINGS
AND COUNTING

IAN KRUGER
THE HAPPY HOTDOG MAN
SOUTHAMPTON, UK

PREPARED FOR PUBLICATION
www.ignitepublishinghouse.com

500 HEALINGS AND COUNTING
BY THE HAPPY HOTDOG MAN, SOUTHAMPTON, UK

Copyright ©July2018 by Ian Kruger

Printed in the United Kingdom

All rights reserved

ISBN-13: 978-1724902689

Published by Ian Kruger

Prepared for publication by Ignite Publishing House
www.ignitepublishinghouse.com

Endorsements

Pastor Andrew White

As you read through this journal your soul will be encouraged, your faith built up and your expectation elevated to new heights. You will see in its pages that Ian has written this journal for one reason and one reason alone to lift up the name of Jesus. Ian is not a man who is concerned about adulation, praise or even acceptance. He has had a genuine encounter with God. That encounter has stirred up a passion to do the works of God. He longs to see lives transformed by a genuine move of God upon individuals that is so tangible it could never be reputed.

Page after page of this journal is filled with stories of broken lives made whole. Many of the miracles you will read about have not happened in a nice comfortable church with an anointed worship team and believers interceding but rather in the day to day situations of life that the Lord has supernaturally orchestrated. Whether it's in a city centre or by a park bench God can change lives if someone will be open to let God use them and step out in faith. Ian is such a person, he has done what so many long to do but have never had the courage to do.

He has learnt to be led by the Holy Spirit. He has learnt to take risks in God, knowing that if he will do the possible God will do the impossible.

This journal is a remarkable example of the love of God that knows no boundaries. People of all ages, backgrounds, creeds and colours have received unconditional love and life altering miracles as Ian has simply been obedient to the direction of the Holy Spirit. It proves to us the readers again and again that God is a good God who does not look on the outward appearance but upon the heart of man.

Ian is known as the happy hotdog man on the streets of Southampton. He can be found day after day by his hotdog stall playing worship music and rejoicing in God. Always with a smile on his face, a listening ear for those in need and ready to pray for any situation he lights up the city centre with the Glory of God.

Many know him as a man of passion for the gospel and a desire to see people saved, healed and delivered but there is another aspect to Ian's life. He is a man who is totally committed to honesty and integrity in life and in ministry. (Even though Ian has made mistakes in the past, he is a man who is totally committed to honesty and integrity in life and in his ministry.) He detests exaggeration and boasting. That's why this journal is written the way it is. The truth the whole truth and nothing but the truth. The stories in this journal are written down just as they happened.

May this journal inspire all of us to be authentic in our faith! To boldly go where few believers have gone before and see God's glory on our streets I wholeheartedly endorse not only this book but also Ian as a man of God.

Pastor Andrew White
Senior Pastor
Victory Gospel Church Southampton

Steve Ryder

I have known Ian for over 30 years and together we have ministered in large scale crusades and have seen the power of God move through crowds of thousands. As I read through this book, I find it just as wonderful to hear of the day-to-day testimonies of the many people that God has touched through Ian's ministry. His humility and genuine love for people make this book a source of inspiration for all.

Dr. Steve Ryder
Reach Out for Christ

Robin Jegede-Brimson

I am delighted to be able to endorse this book by my friend Ian Kruger. I know that it is going to be used to touch people's hearts and stir faith for the miraculous and to see healings on a regular basis. It has been my great joy to hear first-hand over the years from Ian the scores of testimonies of GOD's supernatural intervention in the lives of everyday folk. Ian carries much grace when it comes to healing and a message to The Body of CHRIST that says unequivocally, "YOU CAN DO IT TOO!"

Robin Jegede-Brimson
Servant Ministries
Convenor: Interprophetic Alliance

THE JOURNAL
500 HEALINGS AND COUNTING

THE JOURNAL

July 23rd 2017

Dear Sir, Madam, Ladies and Gentlemen,

To all those reading this and to all those concerned. I have endeavoured to compile into a book a brief journal of healings that have occurred since 3rd January 2005. This is somewhat a sporadic journal, started and stopped in no set pattern over a number of years; and with considerable gaps of time with no record of documented answers to prayer. However, many more healings did occur; even if not recorded. The title of the book is: '500 healings and counting'; even though the true amount is far more than a mere 500, it is more likely to be thousands. I prayed for at least one person a day on average over a period of 12 years. That being a conservative estimate of six thousand people, of which around 50% were healed instantly or within a few days after prayer. Also there were seasons of healing where 90% were most certainly healed instantly after prayer.

The original journal that I wrote by hand was titled 'Look what the Lord has done', so I start this introduction by repeating this statement 'Look what the Lord has done' through me, a simple hot-dog man who at many times has appeared to be totally crazy, the definition of 'a fool' but a fool for Christ Jesus. Indeed, I take no credit at all for the healings recorded in this book, I am simply honoured and overwhelmed within myself that God would use me to touch people's lives in such an innocent yet profound way. That through what many thought was ridiculously way out, over the top and completely wacky at times, God still manifested his love through a touch, a shout, through an obedient act of faith that let heaven touch earth, all to the honour of Jesus.

Let your kingdom come, your will be done on earth as it is in heaven, would become a living reality through a man known in Southampton town centre as "The Happy Hotdog Man". That man is indeed the person who holds this pen, who is trying to truthfully pen this book as an authentic journal kept by myself in a very straightforward way each day in bullet point statement, which would jog my memory when re-read. This is simply a journal, a record, brief statements that within themselves could be expanded into chapters and in reality, will become a great novel of what occurred over a span of approximately 12 years of my life.

This book is in essence a brief summary of healings. Which may also include miracles, signs and wonders (to some sceptics a fabrication, a lie, a big deception) yet with all sincerity after 12 years of keeping these recordings confidential, (apart from a few friends and on the odd occasion to a company of people) I have felt an inward witness of God almighty to now manifest these testimonies through a book.

This book: '500 healings and counting', what God can do through a human vessel simply known as 'The Happy Hotdog Man' in Southampton.

For many years I wondered why these amazing healings and miracles were happening. Why did God instruct me NOT to go through the main media of television, radio, national or local newspapers to testify and share to a mass of people what was happening through me at a street level? Healings were a common everyday lifestyle and the perception of me being weird, eccentric, even a 'fruit loop' was a smoke screen for some pretty amazing happenings. This was no way a coincidence. The personal harassment, intolerance, abuse, discrimination and persecution against me was in actual fact a spiritually orchestrated plan to hinder me ministering Gods Love and healing in public as darkness hates the light. I paid a price on an emotional level to stay obedient to the call of Almighty God, to make a stand against the wicked opposition, to sing, and make a very public declaration that Jesus is alive and loves to touch people through healings today; which he has given me the opportunity to do so; through an obedient and eccentric looking vessel, the shape and form of The Happy Hotdog Man.

So, through much harassment in public and private, seen and unseen, I ministered to thousands in an innocent child-like way. Amazingly, God answered those prayers, more and more and more. What is ironic is that each individual I prayed for who received a healing and a touch from God would have considered themselves 'unique' in the sense of an answer to their specific need. I suppose some may have even in fact be embarrassed to share it with others for the fear of sounding ridiculous. Maybe they had also mocked at the notion that God is personal enough to heal individuals today through a prayer from a Happy Hotdog Man.

Thousands received healing not knowing that they were part of many, and my hope is some of those who had this amazing experience of God's love, will read this book, recognise what has happened, and not be ashamed to acknowledge that God personally became visible to them through a prayer beside a Hotdog cart.

After all these years of remaining relatively silent about the amazing number of healings, a man of God approached me in early July 2017 when I was in Stockport. He said: "You have a book of healings and now is the time to write it." Later on, that month I awoke at approximately 4.00am in the morning, got out of bed, and started writing this introduction. It is now light outside. The dawn of a new day.

This introduction is now complete, I am so grateful that many other people could know and also experience; what I will share through these testimonies. If God can use me to serve others, he can most definitely use anyone who is willing to Love and demonstrate a living resurrected Jesus who desires to heal through those who Jesus died for. Heaven is real, Healings are real, Jesus is real, and Jesus is ALIVE. Get ready to be amazed!

January 3rd 2005

I was completely alone in my room in Millbrook, Southampton. It was my 42nd birthday. Tears rolled down my face. This was not new to me. Tears had been evident almost every day from June 2003 until November 2004. However, this was the first time to what I can recall that there was not one birthday present, not one birthday card. Maybe if there had been just one card from my children then my emotions would have handled it.

As I stood in my room, sobbing, the tears running freely down my face, I lifted my hands to heaven. I made my birthday request to God my father. This was my prayer:

Father God, I thank you for the lovely clothes I bought in the Marks and Spencer sales, they were lovely. For my birthday present, I now ask you to clothe me with some clothing from heaven, in the name of Jesus, give me some of your clothes, of your Holy Spirit. Thank you. Amen.

God heard my prayer. He granted my request. From January 3rd 2005 until April 2005, the Lord allowed me to know and experience a tangible anointing. A presence from the top of my head to the soles of my feet. A real 'Ready Brek' glow.   For ninety days, I experienced something from God that was extraordinary.

Yes, I understand that the anointing will come upon a person and lift of a person as the Holy Spirit wills, however this was God's grace and God's mercy. I believe this was a foretaste of what is to come. For ninety days, every day the Lord clothed me.   The clothing was real, it was heavenly, and it was spiritual. When that continuous anointing/presence/clothing lifted from me, I felt so naked. My spirit-man had become so used to this Holy Spirit covering, he felt unclothed, naked.

I immediately prayed; looked for any sin that might have offended the Holy Spirit. There was no sin evident, so I was puzzled as to why this had happened?

Since then, the tangible anointing has returned on numerous occasions, as the Spirit of God wills, I endeavour to walk in the Spirit every day. I love Father God, I love the Holy Spirit, and I love the Lord Jesus. I desire to know them more and more and more.

I believe the Lord allowed me to experience a covering of the Holy Spirit for a continuous ninety days to show a foretaste of his plan for his people, a glorious church without spot, or wrinkle. Being adorned as a bride for his son's return.

Ephesians 5:27 & 32

In an unusual way, I am quite grateful for no presents, and no cards on my birthday. For as you can see I received, and experienced, the best birthday present ever. Priceless. For ninety days, I was able to influence thousands of people for the Kingdom of God, as the presence of heaven fell around me. As people passed by me, they were aware of a change in the spiritual atmosphere.

I saw many depressed people set free simply by walking through that presence or by coming into contact with me. Many healings took place, almost every day the Lord manifested himself, sometimes in unusual ways. To those who would question these things, or even get jealous, I say to you before God, to the best of my knowledge, I lie not, concerning these memories.

Definition of instant healing: Simply, when a person is prayed for, their healing happens within seconds. Their condition changes rapidly. Many times, swelling and physical symptoms disappear within seconds, stiffness in joints dissipates immediately and they have full movement instantly. If a bone is broken, they have no sign of a broken bone. All pain goes and all movement returns. When this happens, people are in a state of shock and amazement as their natural mind finds it hard to understand or comprehend what has just happened. Many times, when I put down instant healing, this is generally, what has just occurred, and I am just as surprised as the person who has received a dramatic healing. Praise be to God.

Some testimonies from January 2005

1 Lump in breast 'completely gone' after prayer of faith, a prayer of command.   Maureen, Bournemouth.

2 Pain in back 'healed' after hand on shoulder prayer. Pains did not return. 'Leeatt', Jewish Pedlar.

3 Fractured leg healed 'rapidly' in one day, no need for permanent six week cast. Simple prayer, hands on cast, due more to faith of 'Max' a four-year-old boy from Bournemouth. Praise God!

4 Daniel got a good job, with good pay, which he enjoys after prayer of faith.

5 Samantha's ankle 'healed' rapidly after touch on her shoulder and prayer for healing, and a prophetic word of wisdom was also given regarding her future ministry amongst women, etc.

6 Elderly woman in wheelchair could hardly walk, prayer of faith, walking much better with stick.

7 Daniel's 'tonsillitis' healed within two days.

8 Depression lifted off J, after prayer.

9 Christine was gobsmacked as I revealed God had called her into the ministry of an evangelist and prayed a prayer/impartation of that gifting upon her life.

I did not know that The Holy Spirit had spoken to her every day for weeks concerning this matter.   I did not know her from Adam. Her father was an Elder and present while I prayed etc. There is much more to this testimony, space does not permit.

10 Janine's front room, heat in one part of room, during worship time. Raised hands to God in the heat, in worship and adoration, sensed angels up and down into heaven, like Jacob's ladder? To the left of this, I sensed a cloud of witnesses, a portal/balcony, heard an excitement

11

where the cloud of witnesses were, and heard some in heaven saying: 'come look at this'. Interesting?

11 Oppression/depression on Samantha for two weeks, prayed, anointing fell freedom, smiles, laughter, went back to sit on couch. Saw an influence on her neck, ran across the room, spoke 'Release' in Jesus name. Instantly set free of neck pain, which she had not told me about. In addition, the depression started after a horrible dream of a 'hairy monster' embracing her; but God sorted it out.

12 Prayed for Phil's wife, at WCC after an evening meeting, anointing fell, instantly set free of heaviness. Praise God!

13 Michael receives lots of work after prayer of faith. Chap at roofing company (Roof the Ruther), received lots of work within two days of prayer, he was quite desperate! Came back and told me, quite gobsmacked, I did not know this man. This was a word of knowledge etc.

14 Pastor Mark 'preaches' some of his best messages after prayer of impartation, a strong anointing was noticeable during the preaching.

15 Abscess on jaw completely gone after two days, after direct prayer. Steve.

16 Fijians back healed, transferred anointing on woman in red, to pray for her friend, I said, "you pray, you do it", she did, and God honoured it. The back was instantly healed.

17 Pastor Mohan (Sri Lanka) healed of fever. Prayed in the afternoon she was in bed very ill, at breakfast completely restored. Leaders Conference.

18 Specific word of knowledge, I was at a Christian's house warming party. God says, "Don't give up on P just yet." That very afternoon she had said to God "That's it; I'm giving up on P."

19 P felt heat and tangible anointing on hands, as I prayed with my hands underneath his he also felt heat on his shoulders. He was quite puzzled as we were in the car at the time. I saw him trying to work out how heat can pass through a metal roof etc.

20 Saw J face in spirit, I was shocked, discerning of Spirit etc.

21 Met R in shop, she looked down in Spirit, as I talked, and encouraged her, so her countenance lightened up, life and radiance came out of me affecting her Spirit. This was uplifting for me as I was going through some tough tests myself.

22 Paul's chest healed after prayer, difficulty breathing at night for some years. Paul was totally clear after prayer.

23 I was led by the Holy Spirit to be outside West Quay entrance at 1.15pm. I simply knew that I had to be in that exact spot and that exact time. At 1.20pm an elderly woman walked past, tripped, hitting her head on the paving slabs cutting her head open. I instructed the florist, who was talking to me at the time, to put some of the paper napkins on the cut and press hard to stop the flow of blood.

The elderly woman went into 'shock'. Led by the Holy Spirit to simply place my hand on her forehead and release 'PEACE.' Immediately, calmness came on her and over her. She sighed and rested in an assurance that all was well. That rest continued until the ambulance arrived to take her to hospital. Thank you Father God.

24 Blonde woman (Opticians Sales) smoking by side door of shop. I was unloading my van. Holy Spirit said, "She wants to quit smoking; she was talking about it last night. Let her know that if she asks Jesus, he can remove all cravings to smoke, and she will not have to use Nicorette patches." I walked to her and spoke, her attention focussed. I then heard myself say, "You spoke about smoking at about 7pm last night." Her eyes opened wide, her jaw hit the floor, this was completely true etc.

25 Bouncer on the door at King Alfred pub near Saints Football ground. He had severely blocked sinus problem, obviously in much discomfort. I prayed for him publicly in front of the other bouncers. I was expecting instantaneous healing etc. He shrugged his shoulders, indicating that nothing had happened, and I went on my way. Saw him three weeks later. He told me that the next morning when he woke up, his sinuses were completely clear. It scared 'the hell out of him'. Thank you Lord.

26 Ray, arthritic shoulder, instantly set free after prayer/command and working of miracle i.e. getting him to move arm etc. I sensed the evil spirit releasing his shoulder, a big 'yelp' from him as spirit left.

27 Man had lost his voice for six months. Prayed for him publicly, came back one week later. He said that his voice was coming back, and the doctor said that he would make a full recovery in two weeks.

28 Friday Night 10.30pm, driving through Millbrook after meeting with Fijians. Some teenagers were crossing the road by shops. I stopped the car to let them cross. Suddenly, word of knowledge concerning a bad back. Stopped the car, got out and asked them. Was correct. Gift of faith was released. Holy Spirit said, "Do not lay hands on them" so I moved by the gift of faith. Three teenagers wanted healing, so to the teenager who had the painful bad knee I 'slapped' his hand and told him to touch his knee, immediately healed, to the extent that he was stamping his foot on pavement saying "it's real, it's real, it's real" totally amazed. I then immediately commanded the bad back to be 'released' and told the teenage girl to touch her toes three times. (Instantly healed) I slapped girl's hand and told her to lay that hand on the girl's head (where a pair of scissors had hit her, causing a cut, pain and headache.) I asked Jesus for healing, as the girl's hand touched her friend's head the pain left immediately, they were all amazed. They asked if I was God. I replied, "No, this is Jesus flowing through me". Counter attack of enemy as one of the parents arrived ranting, raving and in a foul mood so I left quietly, prayed, and thanked God.

29 BULGARIA – Unwell Saturday, sore throat, runny nose, sneezing etc, forced to go on day trip to mountain restaurant. Did not want to eat. Later I went to the market at the bottom of the mountain. The rest of the team and I separated. Suddenly a gift of faith was released. Started to pray for a woman with bad hips, knees and back. Instantly healed. Then her husband was healed, a crowd lined up for prayer and healing, I prayed loudly and with Holy Spirit boldness. Quite a few people offered me money in payment for their healings which I did not receive but asked them to thank Jesus. I prayed nonstop for approximately 30-40 minutes for people, many were healed instantly. The Bulgarians' called out for prayer. God heard and answered them. Great!

30 The Holy Spirit touches Gillian, as she witnessed this move of God at the market. Later I was able to minister an anointing onto her life, with permission etc. Next day she burst into tears with her mum at the prayer meeting, quite uncontrollable. The Holy Spirit said, "The change has started within both of them." Praise God. By the end of the week, I noticed an increased zeal within Gillian towards God etc. She respected and recognised the anointing. Thank you Lord.

31 BULGARIA– At one point while praying for the sick in a tent meeting, the healings were happening so often and so quick I questioned if the gypsies were making it up. Of course they were not, God's grace and faith was extra special.

32 Quite a few words of knowledge and wisdom released by the Holy Spirit through me to team, plus a wonderful sermon on sowing released to me at 5.00am. Thank you Lord.

33 Holy Spirit visited team in Bulgaria with power for first three days (Monday to Wednesday.) Unfortunately, He was quenched and grieved and was not present in his manifested anointing (Thursday to Monday). Returned, with a manifested presence Tuesday to Friday (second week). Praise God for many instant healings, baptisms in the Holy Spirit and approximately four hundred born again conversations.

One evening, the Roma teenagers received instruction praying for sick, stepped out in faith in main meetings. God moved wonderfully, confirming his word with many healed through the teenagers. Some literally 'shook' as the presence of God flowed through them healing people. They also cried with tears of compassion.   Praise God!

June 29th 2005

34 Word of the Lord spoken by some Angels. Unusual experience, these angels were playful, joyful, almost having fun in a competition in who was going to speak the word first. There is excitement amongst them in the word that is given. Interesting and intriguing.

June 30th 2005

35 The Holy Spirit dictated a prophetic word to me. A follow on from a previous dictation on June 28th 2005 at 7.25am.

July 5th 2005

36 An almost identical re-run of (no 28) testimony. In West Howe, Bournemouth. 'Word of knowledge' for a specific teenager for healing of back, gift of faith. Spoke the Rhema word, slapped hands. Three teenagers instantly healed, all in the space of 5-10 minutes. This happened right outside the house where the house meeting was that I was attending. Perfect timing.

I am expecting the latter part of this year to be greater than the former. This autumn will be special in spirit.

37 Went to tent event, Swanage. After meeting, noticed an older teenager with support strapping round wrist etc. Asked her how long she had had this medical problem. For two years or so, she was receiving physiotherapy had to go for scans, no recovery imminent. I had to coax her into receiving prayer, as she was very shy. She 'asked' Jesus to heal her wrist. I prayed, anointing was quite evident, instantly healed. Removed wrist support, gob-smacked! 'Strength' came back into her very weak wrist; she could grip quite hard for a girl! Her friend, 'Elaine' (middle-aged) received Jesus into her heart, for the first time, and joined in a prayer of agreement for a friend of hers called Lee in Poole Hospital, in a coma etc.

May 28th 2005

38 Man buys hotdog from my cart in Southampton City Centre. His wrists had support straps due to tendons needing surgery etc. Gift of faith. Prayed, wrists healed instantly, pain left immediately, wrists strengthened immediately, quite a strong handshake. Man was gob-smacked and very happy.

August 6th 2006

39 Girl of about eleven years old cast on wrist, soft-top over knuckles. She did not want me to pray for her directly, so I prayed a healing impartation onto her friend's hands, (Gift of faith.) As soon as her friend's hand touched the girl's injured wrist the pain went! The girl was amazed.

40 Prayed for elderly man, (eighty-four years) he was a street-preacher. Cockney walked with stick. Pain in hips, middle and lower back. Prayed, anointing of Holy Spirit flowed, word of knowledge concerning middle and lower back pain, placed my hand there. 'Wallop!'

The Holy Spirit did His fantastic work, man saw me Wednesday 10th– healed completely! No stick preached for three hours without a rest.

Thank you Lord Jesus.

August 8th 2005

41 Worked in Weymouth. Words of knowledge concerning boy on bike (around 11 years old) wanting a free hot-dog with other friends etc. He was getting headaches plus pressure on forehead, also had word of knowledge concerning his friend with torn tendons/wrist (spot on), lad on bike asked me to pray for his hurting ankle/foot so I touched the eighteen year's hand, prayed, told him to place his hand on friend's ankle etc. Pain left ankle immediately, instantly healed. "How did you do that?" he asked. Shared Jesus.

August 13th 2005

42 Prayed for Scottish woman in High Street. I knew her husband from Winchester, growers (bulbs) etc. As I spoke to her, had a word of knowledge concerning her back; pain down middle of spine/back etc. Was that correct? "Yes," "Can I pray for you?" "Yes." Prayed. Instant healing etc. "How did you do that?" she enquired, I witnessed about Jesus etc.

August 19th 2005

43 Mum, Dad and daughter (sixteen years) queued to buy a hot dog. The Lord gave me a word of knowledge concerning the father. "He had an encounter with God that had puzzled him etc." The daughter suddenly exclaimed, "You healed my friend's back!" From this statement I was able to explain it was not me, but evidence that Jesus was resurrected, and his love was displayed via healings, I was also able to share with Father the word of knowledge, the Father confirmed the word of knowledge was true; love and wisdom 'flowed', and they went on their way with much to consider; hallelujah!

August 19th 2005

44 Prayed with 'Jenny' ex-pedlar, Jewish woman (twenty years). She asked Jesus into her life and for the Holy Spirit to reveal himself. 'So let it be.' Amen.

August 20th 2005

45 Prayed for brain-damaged boy 'Liam', and his Gran, Angus (19th– afternoon); led by Holy Spirit to pray at

2.35am (20th) overcome with emotion. Expecting God to do an almighty miracle. Expecting parents to be saved. Expecting to hug a well Liam. Love you Lord, Amen.

That was my hope, faith, expectancy, my God is more than able to do this. Amen.

August 21st 2005

46 Prayed for Chris, (Matthews' friend) he had scars on head and back pain due to a traffic accident plus epileptic fits. His back had improved.

September 2017 update: Never had an epileptic fit since that prayer, praise God.

September 1st 2005

47 Prayed for single mother with children after word of knowledge concerning her sleep problems and fear. Prayer for sweet sleep, immediate manifestation of amazing sleep to the extent that she started to tell all her friends etc.

48 SH (R's husband) asked the Lord into his life after the Holy Spirit instructed me to visit them at exactly

9.00pm. If I had visited at 8.45pm, I would have walked into an argument. I also gave a gift, which demolished the devil's attacks against me. I was in their home from 9.00pm – midnight, was able to witness. Steve asked the Lord into his life early hours of morning. Praise God!

49 The door has opened for me to go to Australia 26th September – 26th October. God has granted me favour. When I spoke to Steve Ryder, I gave him a word that K.K. Chin had also given to him. Amazing. Expecting a great move of God.

September 2nd 2005

50 Oh the faith of the Latter Day Saints woman in her car. Disabled with arthritis in body and short leg since birth. She had seen some youths of who were mucking about near my hot dog cart. I asked her what was wrong with her. She explained, however I knew she had been abused. Arthritis/unforgiveness are linked in this case. I asked her if I could pray for her. She grabbed my hand very tightly with much faith, (**Luke 18:35**) a grabbing faith. Oh, the anointing came upon her heavy, tears in her eyes, tears of gratitude and love. Oh, she should receive! Yes, all arthritis will go from that body. I instructed her to forgive her abusers. I thought she was probably a Christian, from Above Bar Church. She was a Mormon. What faith to receive, God is no respecter of person. The so-called 'non-Christians' are more open to receive God's healing touch than the 'religious' Christians are.

September 6th 2005

51 Lady with heavy period, clots. She was ready to go to the doctor as this had been a problem for some months, allowed me to pray. As I prayed, I saw the light of the Holy Spirit touch her stomach/womb. I knew the healing was released. The woman was open to receive and receive she did. Spoke to her two days later, vast improvement, even a year later no more problems. Praise God.

September 10th 2005

52 Women's ankle instantly healed after prayer of faith. Touched her ankle and prayed at the bottom of the steps by the side of Asda. She was with her husband or boyfriend, about forty years of age. She was totally gobsmacked! I was able to witness and give her a booklet. Amazing.

September 10th 2005

53 Walking to van (Town Centre), about ten youths sitting on wall. Had a word of knowledge that a teenager had a knee problem. A bit of mickey taking by the group, spoke about Jesus. Then I moved in faith and prayed for back pains etc with the teenagers help i.e. hitting hands and asking them to pray for their friends. Three instantly healed of pain. Prayed for fifteen-year-old with paranoia and constant nightmares, sensed a 'release' to his head. He said, 'a weight had left' and smiled.

In addition, a girl prayed for her friend who suffered with asthma, they were all-cool and would consider these events brilliant.

September 7th 2005

54 Four youths were taking a short cut via church car park (Millbrook); one of the teenagers asked me to pray for his injured finger, it was in pain and stiff. I thought he might be joking and ignored his request. Five minutes later, he returned with two friends and asked again. So I prayed. I felt the anointing leave my finger and touch his. He said, "It works!" He was really pleased and walked off. I saw one of his friends on 10th September in town; he was buying a hot dog. I questioned him regarding 7th September. He replied by saying it was genuine and really did work etc. Ha ha ha ha

55 Mark, friend of S and R, back and knees healed. Prayed for him in the afternoon, next morning he was healed.

September 21st 2005

56 Man came to my hot dog cart to say, "I had done him a favour", why. He showed me his arm, from wrist to arm muscle was a scar (stitch) marks. Completely healed of tendon damage after prayer, I shared Jesus etc.

September 21st 2005

57 Walking from van to room (Oldbury Close), three teenagers walking behind me, the Holy Spirit said, "One

29

of them has a bad ankle." I asked, was correct. Gift of faith, prayed, touched lad's hand, he then touched his ankle, instantly healed. Pain went instantly; gob smacked, spoke about Jesus, went indoors and thanked God.

September 23rd 2005

58 Talked with teenagers on Millbrook estate. Lad had painful foot, limping, injured big toe. Asked me to pray. So I prayed with my foot on top of his foot, as led by the Holy Spirit. He said, "Nothing has happened" I replied, "The healing is released". Thirty seconds later, he started to say, "Its better the pain has gone, I can bend my big toe." Amazed he was. Thank you Lord.

September 23rd 2005

59 The Holy Spirit instructed me to approach and anoint with oil around thirty teenagers on the street in Millbrook, Southampton. I asked them if they would like to pray for the sick and see them be healed, in which they replied YES. Not Church goers but very enthusiastic to receive the oil on their hands. (Remember King David was anointed to be a King as a young man many years before he became King).

September 27th 2005

60 Met couple in Tokyo Airport, Christians, Pastor Mark and his mother. Had word of knowledge concerning his mother's bad back. Prayed for her, anointing fell, emotional healing too; anointed her hands for ministry and encouraged them; especially to refocus on Jesus and not church politics.   They were going to Brisbane and knew Steve Ryder.

December 17th 2005

61 Steve Big Issue seller in Southampton. Pain in the head gone after prayer.

62 Young man named Mark (around twenty years), received rapid healing from flu by Asda lifts (Busking) 18th December. Prayed at 11.00am, COMPLETELY BETTER by 5.00pm.   Amazed he was!   Witnessed about Jesus.

December 19th 2005

63 Busker in white, sprayed in silver/white paint. Devon man about fifty years old, with lass, his back healed, "improved" greatly "puzzled" at how I knew he had bad back (word of knowledge). Witnessed about Jesus.

*Lord send miracles, more manifestations of miracles **PLEASE!** Holy Spirit boldness, more sensitivity to you, Oh Lord, help me, I pray.*

December 21st 2005

64 Lady returned to report that her gallstones had disappeared after prayer in the summer; all pain left, no more pain! I was able to pray for her again in regards to a fear of death and oppression. She greatly encouraged me, with her testimony, and excitement. An answer to prayer from God.

65 Woman came back today to say she had received healing to her blocked ears, and depression, when I had prayed for her yesterday (20th December). She then asked me to pray for her again, with her enthusiastic husband, "cheering" and saying "come on" in support. Both these people, (in their sixties) were simple people, with receiving faith that works. Amen.

66 In Australia five people received healing after prayer. Three were healed instantly in a 10-minute time slot, all with pain in the neck etc but overall the healing power did not manifest as in U.K.?

67 Another woman with bad back and walking stick received a 'manifested' healing this afternoon as I moved in the gift of the working of miracles etc. The pain left immediately as I got her to move her back and do what she could not do etc.

68 Angela's daughter received a healing from God over the phone – Australia.

69 R. received deliverance over phone – Australia.

December 23rd 2005

I thank the Lord for all these wonderful testimonies. Of late, there have been some battles regarding a lack of healings etc. It is not me who heals, it is all HIM, JEHOVAH RAPHA, THE HEALING ONE

I submit to Him, I will seek Him, humble myself I will. The enemy of my soul is desperate, fearful of what God is doing to me, in me and ultimately through me, all Glory to God. Amen. I will bless the Lord at all times; His praise shall continually be in my mouth. Get ready for more testimonies.

February 4th 2006

70 Prayed for a man his late twenties. He was hobbling across road on crutches, P and N were in the car at the time and said "Oh no" as I stopped the car to pray for the chap etc. The man had severe pain in his leg, where a serious break had been due to an accident etc. He used to go to Millbrook Christian Centre as a teenager. Anyway, the pain went immediately so we went to Weatherspoon's in Shirley for lunch. Had a word of knowledge for the fifty-year-old bar woman and was able to pray for her shoulder etc.

February 5th 2006

71 Prayed for a man on crutches outside Above Bar Church who was limping. He was with his wife and bought a hot dog. Prayed for leg, pain and stiffness went immediately. Amazed he was.

February 9th 2006

72 Prayed for a young man; so that he could pray for his mother with stomach illness etc. A surge of power went from my hand to his hand as the healing anointing was transferred. He felt it too.

P.S. he came back later to report a healing to his mum.

73 Prayed for others on street; awaiting confirmation of healings if they return to inform etc.

MORE LORD, MORE…. THANK YOU

February 11th 2006

74 Lady who had miscarriage was very happy to say she was expecting.

February 25th 2006

75 A group of teenagers by hot dog cart had a word for sixteen-year-old Sarah; then prayed for backs. Prayed for one girl, I did not lay hands for healing, I commanded the back to be 'loose' in Jesus' name, the pain left 'instantly'. Then I said (out of my spirit) "your back is shaking" (it was). The spine was vibrating as the bones and discs moved into their correct position. Very easy. Just the spoken word 'backed up' by the Holy Spirit. Thank you Lord. The girl was amazed and open to hear about Jesus, with her friends listening too etc.

February 26th 2006

76 Prayed for Malcolm (Landlord) stomach ulcers. By March 6th he was off all medication. Healed? He was sceptical if it was due to prayer. Umm.

March 3rd 2006

77 Prayed for twenty-year-old man. Severely damaged wrist. He bought a hot dog, allowed me to pray for wrist. (To humour me I think.) Anyway, I prayed asked God to heal his almost broken wrist – lots of pain evident. A gift of faith hit me, so I said "move your wrist" he responded "you don't understand, it's almost broken, pain, stiff etc…" I said, "Move your wrist". He replied, as at first, "you don't understand…."   I replied in a loud and authoritative voice "move your wrist" he moved his wrist and swear words were spoken in amazement and shock, wrist completely pain-free and full movement. He walked off with friend in absolute amazement. Gob smacked!

March 9th 2006

78 Prayed for man in Palm Court Hotel, Malta. Back had improvement after two days.

March 16th 2006

79 Was able to pray for Mary on plane, she was seated next to me. Arthritis left her neck immediately plus full movement etc. Was able to talk to her about Jesus and heaven for one hour. She was a Catholic woman. Thank You Lord.

March 21st 2006

80 Was able to pray for Alan injured etc. at work. After two days, no pain, plus full movement. He commented on it in the kitchen. Thank You Lord.

81 Jamie, street entertainer (silver statue) moves when money is put into his collection box etc. had a deep cut on his finger that was not healing due to location. Prayed. Two days later it started to knit together and heal quickly. Really spoke to Jamie.

82 Man came back to share of healing to his shoulder; now believes in God and Jesus!

April 30th 2006

83 Prayed for teenage girl, who had a sty in her eye. Felt wind of the Holy Spirit rush past my hand as I prayed, she felt this too. She returned one week later to say it had virtually disappeared and she would have to cancel surgery. I told her to 'thank Jesus' which she had done. Thank You Jesus.

May 3rd 2006

84 Woman from Ireland with partner bought two hot dogs. Looked at her, saw she had problems mentally; by the gift of the Holy Spirit. Talked with her, asked her what Jesus could do for her? She asked, 'give me luck?' I replied, 'what about healing?' She said that she suffered from an unusual form of depression. I asked if I could pray. She said 'yes'. I placed my hand on her shoulder, "Father God in the name of Jesus..." instantly I discerned the evil spirit lifting off her and flying off. She felt it lift off her head as I 'saw' it leave. I kept my hand there and the Holy Spirit filled her. Big smile and release all over her face. I said, 'you received more than a hot dog; you will no longer have depression.' Off she went.

May 11th 2006

85 Went into motorbike shop in Winton, Bournemouth. Biker Dave had an arthritic wrist with 'support bandage', in pain and stiff. Led by the Holy Spirit with gift of faith. Prayed, instant healing and full movement in wrist. He had faith in Jesus but did not go to

39

church. Also prayed for owner of shop; she suffered from migraine and bad back etc. The Holy Spirit was evident. She opened up to say she was a Christian and had attended an Elim church for three years. Thank You Lord.

86 Chinese woman returned to hot dog cart to say that 'all the Eczema' had left her hands after praying for her last Saturday (6th May 2006). Brand new skin. She was a Buddhist but now believed in Jesus.

May 19th 2006

87 Second teenage girl returned to say her sty in the eye had gone rapidly after praying for her.

May 18th 2006

88 Christian woman returned to say her friend's back was healed after a 'word of knowledge' and prayer etc.

May 26th 2006

89 Woman phoned to say that God had healed her at Wolverhampton meeting the previous Sunday; I saw her womb open up during that Sunday meeting, Monday she was no better; Tuesday totally healed! Word of knowledge came to me after dancing around Cinema/Church due to obedience of Holy Spirit etc. Michael's church.

90 Prayed for Louis for ongoing cough. Anointing flowed. Completely healed two days after. Yippee! Thank You, Lord.

91 Michelle's back healed. Ruth saw the Holy Spirit ministering to her friend etc. Thank You Lord. I also saw the same by the Holy Spirit.

June 1st 2006

92 Prayed for eighteen-year-old girl in the phone shop. She had a broken wrist in a temporary cast. Chinese rep started to mock, so I told him to 'shut up'. He did. Next day no sign of break as she went to hospital for permanent cast. Miracle. Thank You Jesus.

June 8th 2006

Most unusual word "I will take great delight in exalting (you) as an anointed horn and raising you up."

June 26th 2006

93 Lad with weak eye who never did return after prayer; but the two girls who were with him had sties and were completely healed. Praise God. His brother told me a few days ago that the eye healed up two weeks after prayer and is okay.

June 22nd 2006

94 Gypsy woman's back healed instantly after prayer by West Quay entrance, loud command in Jesus name of 'loose' etc. She was 'cool' about it.

June 29th 2006

95 Jamie street performer (statue) (Southampton City Centre); brought his girlfriend for prayer to her hand. Scar on hand due to operation, plates by thumb etc. Stiff and pain, 'loose' prayer etc. Immediate movement and pain free, stunned she was. Jamie smiled at her and said, "Told you!"

June 29th 2006

96 Elderly woman in wheelchair; 'lung disease' (Emphysema) Prayed, anointing poured into her lungs, strong manifestation, expecting a total healing. Looking for a good report etc. Thank You Lord.

June 29th 2006

97 Impartation of 'healing anointing' to Christian woman; also Daniel's dad also received a touch from God! No arthritis in his blood after doctor's tests. Yippee!

98 In town today, woman with strap on thumb. Arthritis and in pain. Prayed, immediately healed. Surprised.

July 6th 2006

99 God's anointing fell on me today as I went into town with hot dog cart. I prayed for an alcoholic who had pneumonia on his lungs; prayed with authority 'loose', God's spirit touched the man like wind. Praise God, he knew the manifested touch of God as his lungs cleared.

Confirmation from Australia (February 2007)

100 Woman came back to report a testimony of healing to her heart due to previous prayer etc. Overjoyed she was as she thought she was a goner.

July 7th 2006

101 Elderly woman Jean returned to 'ask' for healing to her neck. After prayer last time, she did not need calliper for her leg. Her leg was out of shape and needed a calliper/brace to keep it straight. The leg straightened out overnight. Doctor was amazed. The Lord touched her neck, lots of heat etc. Half an hour later there was significant movement in her neck, she had faith to believe for her neck brace to be removed by the end of the week. Her husband was very emotional. Thank You Lord. (By the end of the week no neck brace was needed, she had no pain and full movement restored.)

July 8th 2006

102 Met Barry, (Daphne's son) a South African. Reported that his hip was completely better after prayer three days ago. The anointing flowed into his hip, causing a healing and a cure. Praise God, more miracles and healings! Increase.

July 28th 2006

103 Mother and daughter returned to report wonderful healing. When I saw them, last the daughter was hobbling on crutches. I was led by the Holy Spirit to pray for the daughter of twelve years after permission from the mother. I took the crutch, placed it on the ankle, and prayed. The anointing flowed. After leaving, they carried on shopping. Within half an hour the swelling went down, all pain left, the bruising disappeared (vanished) and the girl was able to walk unaided! A sign and wonder indeed. Praise God, thank You.

"Start to encourage people to speak to Jesus." A High Street message. Umm, "you" speak to Jesus; then he will become real. Millions of angels ready to minister to people of Southampton etc.

August 26th 2006

104 A black woman and two children in car near to where I was led to put on some Christian music to witness. As I was about to push hotdog cart into the High Street, I was led by Holy Spirit to walk by the woman, she asked me to help her, "have you some milk for my gastric stomach, I'm in a lot of pain." I replied, "sorry no milk, but can I pray for you?" "Yes," so I prayed, hands on stomach etc. Anointing fell, instantly healed. She said: "Now I know you are a man of God." Amen. Thank You Lord.

August 20th 2006

105 Lady in a wheelchair (approximately in her early twenties), had hurt her back severely previous day. Led to pray for her. Encouraged her to stand. Holy Spirit said, "Command a release on her back", umm I thought, anyway I shouted 'release' to her back in Jesus' name. The pain left immediately, instant healing. I walked her to a pedlar who had earlier that day called me 'a div' for playing music too loud and praying for people. Umm.

106 Prayed for man (in his thirties) who had broken wrist-playing cricket. He was out of cast but had a support bandage on. Needed five weeks of physiotherapy to regain full movement. Prayed, within ten seconds his wrist was okay. He was in a state of shock and a state of amazement. I asked him to tell the Flower Seller, he said "faith healer, wrist, movement ..." I said, "thank you Jesus".

107 Headache instantly healed (Jordan). Told him to move his neck too and that the pain would go (word of knowledge). J, K, S, R, J present (five again).

108 On the way to my room, a young woman of about nineteen years healed instantly of a headache after witnessing about Jesus/Heaven. Clicked fingers as directed to by Holy Spirit; in front of her friends. By the Holy Spirit I knew exactly where the pain was on her head; she denied this initially, but later admitted this was so. Able to witness.

109 Man (in his thirties) healed of a neck condition that he had suffered with for seven months. Happened in a Jacuzzi. He was shocked. 'Release' prayer.

110 Elderly woman instantly healed of upper spine pain (worsening it was) in Bournemouth Gardens car park. She was from Switzerland, husband in a home. She prayed every night, went to church faithfully each Sunday in Switzerland. Had been in prayer for pain/neck problem etc. Praise God.

111 Young man named B, (in his twenties) came back 7th September to report an amazing healing/miracle to his finger. That is approximately two months after prayer. The doctor/surgeon said he would lose his finger due to it being black and dead due to injecting heroin into it. If they could save it; then there would be no feeling in it; as the limb was dead including all the nerves, after prayer a creative miracle took place, all feeling was restored; plus the life of God; a resurrected finger. Hallelujah.

September 12th 2006

112 Prayed for a Russian man's hand, broken knuckles etc. Felt pain due to arthritis in hand, especially in winter; returned to say his hand is better, healed! Praise God; hallelujah.

"Thank You Father God".

September 21st 2006

113 Jewish pedlar's back instantly healed today as I held his hand and prayed. Really spoke to him, I directed him towards Elohim as he was an 'agnostic Jew' etc. Tears in his eyes.

September 21st 2006

114 Older teenager returned to say his wrist had healed; "it works," he said. I got him to "Thank Jesus". Amen.

115 D and M's dad (John) filled with Holy Spirit at approximately 11.15pm umm. Praise God.

September 22nd 2006

116 Young man's neck instantly healed; after word of knowledge and prayer. By hotdog cart.

117 (see also 101 and 124) Elderly woman Jean returned today for more prayer. No need for calliper on her leg. No pain in back when she goes to bed. She had suffered pain for many years. I shared Jesus with her, prayed for her hand. To my amazement, the Lord gave her a miracle; the hand had full movement and pain free. She had had tendonitis for twelve years, which two operations had failed in curing etc. The lump on her thumb/knuckle went instantly. Her husband cried as he saw this miracle. Thank You Lord.

September 27th 2006

118 Another young man returned to say his broken wrist was "healed" after prayer, astonished he was. Resulting in no need for a permanent cast.

September 29th 2006

119 P, my son, healed instantly of a very sore throat, which he had had for a few days. This was a significant sign to him, as a religious education teacher at school had attacked his faith. His fingertips got hot as I prophesied a healing ministry into his life as directed to by the Holy Spirit.

October 13th 2006

120 Lad had operation to remove wisdom teeth (a week ago) lots of pain, plus bruising to jaw. He told me at the hotdog cart, so I prayed for him, laying hand near the affected area. Immediate healing. He was gob smacked, able to share Jesus, and told him this was a sign of Jesus and his resurrection etc. Amen.

October 28th 2006

121 Prayed for eighteen-year-old woman who had a bandage on her hands due to burns, redness and scab, in a lot of pain. Therefore, I prayed and asked her to move hand; all pain left apart from thumb, so prayed again. ALL pain gone, full movement. Praise Jesus.

122 On my way back to room witnessed to a group of teens (late teens). One had a severely bruised ankle, so I imparted an anointing onto his friend's hand and instructed him to place hand on friend's ankle. Within one minute the ankle was healed. Witnessed about Jesus.

November 1st 2006

123 Woman of approximately fifty years, standing in queue at Asda, (Southampton); word of knowledge concerning her back. Lower pain in spine, plus weak back, spoke to her at entrance. Held her hand, prayed, anointing flowed on her 'like oil'; also flowed from my arm. She also felt the power of God flow into her body. She noticed the healing immediately, pain left, straightened back etc. Gave her some Gospel booklets and information about Victory Church.

124 (see also 101 and 117) John and Jean returned 1st November to receive more prayer. Her two daughters burst into tears when they saw the miracle to her hand.

One has been a nurse for many years at Southampton hospital.

Update from Jean on 12/3/2011: Jean who has not walked for around forty years, got out of her wheelchair and walked around the hot dog cart.

November 2nd 2006

125 After praying for woman in High Street, with arthritis in her knees a Jewish woman peddler (around eighteen years) requested prayer for her back. As I prayed, I asked Jesus to heal her neck too. She said she also had pain in her neck. She did not like me praying in Jesus' name, as she loves Elohim. I explained Elohim is the healer etc. She felt the anointing of the Holy Spirit. God's healing touch.

126 Young woman in her early twenties returned to say that I had given a word of knowledge regarding depression etc. I then prayed, laid hand on her head etc. depression "left" her, now she has a job and some other wonderful things, she had previously been out of it!! The anointing of the Holy Spirit not only healed her, but so totally motivated her and helped her to get a job, a big thing for her. Hoorah, Praise God.

November 8th 2006

127 Eighteen-year-old man bought hot dog. His small finger was strapped to the next finger. Broken, bruised, considerable pain. Prayed thanking God for his healing. "Bones knit rapidly, pain go in Jesus' name". To my amazement, the pain left his broken finger and he moved them without any prompting from me. "I couldn't move my fingers, what did you do?" I explained Jesus is alive and not a fairy story etc. Praise God. Joy.

128 Gypsy woman came to hot dog cart to buy hot dog with friend and children. She had pain in her stomach due to ulcer. By the gift of word of knowledge, I knew exactly where the pain was. 'Rebuked' the ulcer and commanded 'the pain' to go in Jesus' name; I knew the spirit of infirmity leaving, so did all the pain, instantly. Praise God.

November 8th 2006

129 Old woman with arthritis in hip, with walking stick instantly healed. Hip loosed up, happy she was after loud 'rebuke' and 'loose' in Jesus' name. Praise God thank You Lord.

I noticed a considerable increase in the anointing after Bev Victory/Community Church instructed me to pour oil over myself in the shower as a sign of fresh anointing. It took me three-four weeks to follow these instructions, Holy Spirit instructions.

November 9th 2006

130 Prayed for a man (in his twenties) who had a cast on his hand and wrist (temporary cast). Had broken wrist and fingers a few days earlier. Heat! God's power touched his wrist and fingers. He was able to move fingers, no pain etc.

November 10th 2006

131 Christian man headache and eyes blurred, healed instantly.

132 Prayed for young woman (nineteen years) after word of knowledge. 'Pain in stomach'. "How did you know?" etc. Rebuked the pain 'loudly' in Jesus' name, it left immediately. Told her about Jesus.

November 12th 2006

133 Man (eighty-two years) bought hot dog with Christian daughter. Asked me if I could pray for her dad. She said his vision was blurry. So laid hands on his eyes, rebuked spirit of infirmity and asked Jesus for healing. Took hands away the eighty-two-year-old said he could see clearly. Praise God.

November 15th 2006

134 In Asda, prayed for a woman shelf-filler who had a bad back. I put my hand exactly where the pain was; sensed God's healing touch, flowing into her back. Also spoke to the 'trapped nerve' loose in Jesus' name, pain went etc. Magnified Jesus. Amen.

November 17th 2006

135 Lad of approximately thirteen years with his Mum, bought hot dog, noticed cast on his hand. Asked about it. Temporary splint cast. Broke fingers two days previously. Asked his mum if I could pray for him if he agreed. Yes. So prayed asking God the Father to rapidly heal his bones and commanded pain to go. Asked the lad what was happening?   "Feels good, feels good" he replied. Therefore, I asked him to move his fingers.   All pain was gone.   Full movement instant healing and miracle, shared Jesus with them, they were amazed.

November 11th 2006

136 The Holy Spirit told me that God the Father was desiring to see people healed and to see miracles 'more, even more, much more' than me, or anyone else! I saw a sun trying to burst/break through some clouds i.e. God's desire to heal and bring miracles into people's lives.

Praise God.

November 23rd 2006

137 Julie and husband (Millbrook Towers) came to buy hot dog. I noticed temporary cast on his hand up to his elbow; he had broken his finger punching a wall two days previously. Therefore, I said, "Ok good, God will heal you" quite bold; as I had an excitement in my spirit so prayed expecting a miracle and a miracle happened there and then. He was absolutely amazed etc.

November 28th 2006

138-143 Five miracles in one hour.

Feeling pretty naff today, pain in colon (kidney stones), cancelled contact with Peter and Nathan, went to Poole to pray for William who has had a serious problem with his only kidney. I was going to ask them to forgive, pray and return to my room and go to sleep etc. I arrived, had a nice cup of tea, and talked to Will, Angela, Matthew, Brianna etc. I knew that the power of God had come into the room. I believe this was a visitation from God, an angel or even Jesus, the presence of heaven filled the room. I shared some testimonies and exalted Jesus.

Two people visited unexpectedly, and the phone rang twice (fowls of the air trying to hinder the work of God). Anyway, there was peace, so we all held hands and invited the Lord to heal, deliver and 'forgive' us all for unforgiveness etc.

First, I prayed for B, the fire of God touched the top of her head, she was amazed at God's tangible presence, then I prayed for A the oppression lifted off her immediately, and then I prayed for M. The fire of God touched his lungs, the asthma left immediately 'the rasp' left immediately; the lung was 'loosened' immediately etc. Prayed for 'fire' to come on M's hands 'to heal' etc.

Then I prayed for Will, he had not been able to walk properly for ten months, the renal failure caused his blood to be filthy, calcium and nutrients were not getting into his body. M's hands were hot after impartation of Holy Spirit. Three years previously, I had prophesied that M would pray for the sick and his hands got hot then, like now etc.

Therefore, I laid hands on Will's kidneys as the Holy Spirit instructed, and asked M to lay his hands on Will's shoulders etc. As M did this, the power of God came on him and flowed through him.

After prayer I said "come on let's test this out" to his wife's utter amazement Will started marching up and down their kitchen, completely healed, life and energy (energy) permeated his body, his face glowed. No pain, walking totally unaided, also, the blotches left his face. Joy and laughter filled the house. To God is the glory... Brianna received Jesus, was filled with the Holy Spirit "all pain" left her stomach (which she had not mentioned).

I then prayed over phone for Julie Ann, who was healed. Her baby glowed as she laid hands on him (two years) in line with Holy Spirit's instruction. I saw God smile, so that boy will be okay, even though he has never talked in two years.

Five miracles in one hour, then M and Will went outside to go to Asda, they rushed back inside, excited, they reported a clear circle of sky over the house, where all around for miles was rain, clouds and darkness. This was at night time (8pm). Thick black clouds. God had given a sign in the sky, a portal - open heaven. Heaven had invaded earth in a most wonderful way. Umm?

November 29th 2006

144 Lad, (Nineteen years) with broken knuckle. Broken previous day, had taken two months to heal as he had broken it previously, I prayed in faith, God healed his knuckles instantly.

November 29th 2006

145 Woman (Twenty years old approximately) had curvature of spine plus hip and joint pain. Prayed to 'Loose' the spine in Jesus' name, tingling etc. Prayed for hip then I got her to touch her toes, which she previously could not do, etc. Healed!

146 Young woman (20-25) Danish pancake seller, pain in feet and legs constantly. Holy Spirit instructed me to tell her to place her feet on top of my feet. Prayed. Pain left immediately. She was amazed. Praise God.

61

God is up to something special.

November 30th 2006

147 Young man with the build of a rugby player forward, came hobbling along on some metal crutches. Ankle severely damaged, acute pain/swollen etc. Asked him if he wanted to be healed? Yes, he replied. The Lord instructed me to get on my hands and knees and pray for his ankle; to lay hands on his ankle, which I did. I knew, that I knew, that I knew, that God had healed him instantly. Therefore, I got up, and asked him to move his ankle. To his utter amazement, the ankle was completely healed and pain free. He shouted at me, "What did you do?"

I immediately took the crutches off him; walked him up and down without his crutches. He was so overjoyed he gave me a bear hug. I encouraged him to 'thank Jesus'. He told two people what happened before walking off, carrying his crutches. Praise God.

November 30th 2006

148 Woman came along with walking stick with hubby in their fifties. I asked if she was in pain. Yes, after knee surgery. Prayed, pain left immediately. Bemused they were. Umm.

December 6th 2006

149 Teenage girl (Sixteen years) from Northam area asked for a free hotdog. She thanked me for a healing to her hand previously. Then asked for prayer to her injured neck, bruised, stiff and in pain. Therefore, I asked her to ask Jesus to heal her neck. She did. I placed my hand on her shoulder. I did not pray, as I knew Jesus was healing her neck as I sensed the presence of the Holy Spirit touching her neck. All I said was "start to move your neck side to side". As she did all the stiffness left, all the pain left.

I asked her to say "thank you" to Jesus etc. She emotionally asked, "How did you do that?" so I explained that Jesus did it, she replied "yes, but how did you do that". I explained Jesus did it. She asked the question three more times.   Therefore, I finally said, "Jesus loves you so much he answered your prayer".   The penny dropped, the revelation hit her that Jesus is alive, and tears filled her eyes that Jesus cares for her and had healed her.

December 7th 2006

150 (see also 146) Yesterday, there was a confrontation with the German Market beer tent/hot dog seller etc. A German woman trader started to shout at me concerning my music.   The next day (today) I was asked to pray for German hot dog seller who hurt his knee badly, twisted, pain, hobbling.   Danish pancake woman had told him about her healing.   So I prayed for this new age follower, behind the pancake stall.   I laid hands on his knee and prayed.   Holy Spirit asked me to get him to move his knee.   The knee was instantly healed.   I was amazed and happy because it was him.   Yes, praise God. He was into new age healing – chi force self-healing, reads many books on the subject and could not understand how the healing could happen so rapidly.   He was amazed.   I gave him a Christian book to read about healing by

Kenneth E. Hagin.   Praise God, the Lord is on his

Thank you Jesus.

December 7th 2006

151 Teenage lad (Seventeen years old) had stitches in his lip, had been in pain for 6 days. I prayed for his hand in front of a group of other teens who were with him. I then asked him to touch his lip.   The pain went immediately from his lip. It freaked him out, even though he had granted me permission to pray etc. A sign and a wonder etc. the expression on his face was classic, as he was not expecting anything to happen!

December 7th 2006

152 Prayed for a woman in a wheelchair with lupus. Strong presence of the Lord. Interesting because some months previously the man who was pushing her wheelchair had a very aggressive outburst towards me as I was unloading my van. (Dragon-headed walking stick)

December 8th 2006

153 Eighteen year old lad; had temporary cast on hand to his broken thumb. He was meant to have permanent cast on Monday 11th. Prayed, Holy Spirit touched bones, knitted rapidly. I hit his cast very hard, no pain, healed, thank you Jesus. The break to the thumb was so severe that he was told that after six weeks of permanent cast he might still require an operation for metal plates etc. That is before the miracle!

154 Prayed for Henry's shoulder, tighter.

December 14th 2006

155 Went into town centre for walk; the council has confiscated my hot dog cart. The German hot dog seller asked if I could pray for his friend (cartilage injury to knee) (see 150). Anyway, the Holy Spirit said to me "I will heal him" so I replied to the new age man "he will be healed". Half an hour later, I prayed for his friend, a loud command in Jesus' name 'loose' the knee was healed and pain free (instantly).

The knee had been in pain for weeks previously. \
a wonderful testimony, especially as I was not able
work and could have been bitter about it.   Praise God.

December 16th 2006

156 Woman bought a hotdog from me with arthritic
fingers and wrists, she had surgical supports on both
hands and wrists.   I asked her if I could pray, "Yes" so I
prayed.   The Lord allowed me to know exactly what he
was doing as I prayed.   I asked her to remove all supports
and strapping, she was totally pain free, healed, full
movement in fingers and wrists. Praise God.   Missed it
a little, when I threw the supports onto C's trolley and told
her the woman would not need them anymore.   C. has
constantly opposed the work of God in the town centre.

December 17th 2006

157 Millbrook lad at Christmas Carol Service healed of
painful injured toe.   Thank you Jesus.

December 17th 2006

158 Chinese takeaway round S and R. Prayed for Linda, swelling on jaw went down instantly, pain left; this was at the dinner table. The fire of the Holy Spirit healed her. Later that evening she received Jesus into her life ha ha ha. R led her into a prayer of salvation. Praise God. Eva also had a healing to stomach at the table. The presence of the Lord was present to heal. Interesting visitation?

159 Man bought hot dog, obviously in back – pain. Therefore, I asked if I could pray, "yes" so loud prayer. The sciatica left immediately, he had been in constant pain. Healed etc. Praise God.

December 20th 2006

160 Woman returned to say 'thank you' for reconciliation with her friend, after a big falling out. She was Hindu or Asian. I had prayed for her previously in regards to this matter. God is no respecter of person, but He respects faith and loves to answer child-like prayers.

December 24th 2006

161 Lad (eighteen year old) hobbled up to buy hot dog with girlfriend. Injured foot, much pain. Asked if I could pray for him. Yes. So put hand on foot and prayed. Asked God to heal and take pain away. Got up, asked lad if pain was there; as he moved his foot he went bright red and said all pain was gone. He was astonished, his brain could not figure out what had happened. His girlfriend laughed as he told her etc. Ha ha, praise God, thank you Jesus.

January 5th 2007

162 Woman (twenties) who was healed of stomach pains/condition brought a woman friend (forties) with her who had severe back pains. She said, "You won't be able to do anything for me!" However, the Holy Spirit through the 'gift of faith' had told me he was going to heal her instantly. 'Loose' in the name of Jesus; instantly healed, back had complete healing, free of pain, free in movement. God had set her free from a spirit of infirmity that had bound her body. By the Holy Spirit I knew it was 'a spirit' causing the condition, the anointing of God caused me to shake as I prayed and after. Praise God.

May 8th 2007

163 Four Macedonian gypsies tried to sell me 'gold' jewellery. They had some hotdogs. I then prayed for the mother who had gastritis in her stomach. Instantly healed, all pain left immediately after a loud rebuke of this stomach complaint. I was able to pray for the baby who was ill at their home. The baby's mother had lots of faith as she saw what had just happened to her mother. I prayed the prayer of agreement with her. Praise God.

164 A young woman of around eighteen years was passing my hotdog cart with people that I had previously prayed with. This young woman had water on her eye and was in pain. She requested prayer, so the Holy Spirit instructed me to get her to put her hand on top of mine and asked me to praise and worship to my music player. Which I did. When I knew the anointing was on her hand, I asked her to place her hand on her eye and count to ten. Which she did. Instant healing to her. Amazement. Her friend said: "Its magic!" Well I suppose its Gods magic instead of Harry Potter magic. It's not 'Black magic', but Holy Spirit heaven touching earth.

Here we have the gifts of the Holy Spirit operating together and flowing one into another. The gift of faith, the gift of the word, of knowledge, the gift of discerning of spirits and finally the power of God manifested to remove pain and instantly heal the back, all in a split second.

This all happened naturally, I was not in control of what was happening I simply yielded to the Holy Spirit with child-like obedience and faith. You cannot control the Holy Spirit, He must lead you and that means trusting His leading, simply 'obey His instructions' in praying for the sick etc.

Training programmes to minister to the sick are good. However, Jesus ministered in many 'different' ways to many people. There are no healing formulas so to speak. "For as many as are led by the Holy Spirit are the sons of God".

Hearing God and then moving in faith is the way of the Holy Spirit. Without faith it is human reasoning, intellect, turns into formula, which in turn becomes 'religious' and tries to control God.

The evidence of the anointing is demonstrations of healings, miracles, signs and wonders, deliverances, the kingdom of God manifested openly, the counterfeit is proud people doing it their way, looking spiritual, looking decent and proper, doing it 'decently and in order' and very little happens. However, I know that the Lord is 'yearning' for those of a right heart motive to increase in His anointing to pray for the sick and to see the sick healed.

The Lord wants to demonstrate that His Son is 'ALIVE'.

It is my understanding that God's healing is given to show God's love, grace and mercy. It is who God is. When church leaders see healings, miracles etc as a way to promote church growth (which is in itself good) they have 'missed' the heart of God. God will heal a sick person if they become a Christian or not; healing is not conditional. It is by grace, unmerited, unearned favour. Simply put God does not heal so churches can grow. However, a by-product of miracles is church growth. God does not heal because the person ministering is mature spiritual etc. No, God heals because of His love for that sick/hurting person. God heals with 'no strings' attached; with no other motive than pure love. May we love the same! Love, love, love...

January 21st 2007

165 Two young men (in their early twenties) talking by Bargate entrance near Post Office. One of the men had his hand in a cast; I spoke to him about it; he had pins in his hand three weeks previously; was in considerable pain and could not move three of his fingers. So prayed "commanded" rapid healing and pain to 'go' in Jesus' name. Asked how his hand was. He laughed in amazement as his hand had instant full movement and all the pain had gone. His skinhead friend was also amazed. I then asked the man to say 'thank you to Jesus' which he did. I then went on my way. Praise God. Interesting.

January 25th 2007

166 Two 'down and outs' came along. One man and one woman. The man was pushing the woman in a wheelchair. The woman in the chair had one leg. The man had an infection in his ankle, pain in his hip and knee, knee very stiff, limited movement etc. They were so dirty and smelly I was reluctant to pray for them. I prayed for the man first; the pain left the ankle, hip and knee. I encouraged the man to move his leg/knee to my amazement the leg healed there and then. He was so pleased, chuffed he was, spoke to him about Jesus. I also prayed for the woman in chair as her only leg was quite swollen.

Therefore, this is a journal of what the Lord has done through a Christian hot dog seller. There will be much more to come...

Seriously, it is not hard to see the sick healed. I have been obedient to the Lord's instruction in keeping a record of these events.

You too can do these things and even greater works. This is only the beginning. 'Elementary dear Watson…'

This is 'child's-play' to what God is going to do through His glorious church.

In finishing this part may I quote the words of prophet 'Nike' "just do it!" and as you step out in faith, as you pray for the sick, as you get a compassion for the hurting, as you keep 'asking' God to heal through you, as you desire the Holy Spirit to minister through you, so it will happen. Keep pressing in until healings happen daily through you; then 'rejoice' in what the Lord has done because He is good, He is God, and he has used you to reveal His love and glory. Amen.

Also read Luke 6 repeatedly because with 'the glory' comes the suffering. Praise God.

The sufferings over the past two years have been many; gossip, slander, mocking, harassment, threatening, temptations, discouragement, sleepless nights, a 6 month hate campaign, isolation, rejection, misunderstanding, tears etc.

Alongside all these trials, temptations, tests, persecutions, have been some wonderful revelations of the Holy Spirit, visions, impartations, prophetic words by recognised anointed prophets 'confirming' God's word, the spirit of revival manifesting, open heavens, angelic visitation, God's favour.

The Lord has shown me great favour; he has shared with me of some of the great things to come. He has shared some secrets with me. I know some of what is to come.

I will leave you with a thought: - the glorious church Ephesians 5:27 are not even in its infancy stage; actually, it has still to be birthed? The glorious church will be birthed out of the present church; the great outpouring of the Holy Spirit and the great harvest that accompanies that, will cause God's desire of an end time church that will outshine the early church of the book of Acts. The best wine is kept for last. The glory of the latter rain and 'the temple' is far, far greater than anything ever seen, or experienced before. In January 2005, the Holy Spirit clothed me for 90 days; an amazing experience yet that *are only a foretaste of what has to come. These testimonies are to inspire, to encourage you to do the same; ye are infant in comparison to what every believer will walk into; as the literal glory (Shekinah) clothes his sons. Alone with the covering of Shekinah is a cloak of humility, a wonderful cloak.*

There is so much more, more than many realise, or understand. Jesus is the author and finisher of our faith.

Amen

The journal restarts…

July 20th 2008

167 Town centre, Southampton. Young man of around eighteen years, his knee at ninety degree angle Dislocated bad!!! Prayed and laid hands on knee; off he went with Girlfriend. Woke up next morning 'completely' healed to the extent he took the leg brace off. HEALED. His Girlfriend reported this to me in front of two Police officers. Thank you Jesus.

July 24th 2008

"Radical-obedience" sets you apart.

When the flesh and mind say "NO" yet the Lord says "YES". It's not following the status-quo and is not seen as "normal".

Radical-obedience is extremely pleasing to God. Lord help me to become "Radically-obedient" Thank you.

August 3rd 2008

168 Went to work outside Above Bar Church. Two people begging; so I said: "Have you ever cracked a rib?"

The woman said: "Yes I cracked my rib four days ago" So I prayed, and The Lord healed her 'Instantly'. The woman was thankful and wants to go to Church.

169 Israeli pedlar who 'mocked me' concerning a dispute on how they were working outside West Quay entrance. God vindicated righteousness and his name. They seemed shocked! Reminded me of the Israeli lesbians who mocked God in Southampton centre. (Pedlars etc..) Thank you Lord God almighty.

170 A miracle in getting clearance for my pedlar certificate. Amazing favour.

171 Man healed instantly as I laid hands on him in PM meeting at Church. Neck/head pains etc..

August 8th 2008

172 Kicked off last night at the football match, Stoke. Outside the King Alfred pub. Prayed for 3 woman. A mum in her fifties and daughter and one other woman in her late twenties. Word of knowledge for the Mum: Lower back bottom of spine. Then woman with crutch, knee arthritis/ hole in back of knee also. The daughter was a heroin addict. Then it kicked off with this black man who had been manifesting to steal what God was doing. Shouting, aggressive, turned into a major brawl with four bouncers. The landlady of The King Alfred and the partner of the heroin addict all saw the kingdom of God in action, manifested publicly for all to see. Interesting?

August 9th 2008

173 The daughter from yesterday came to my hotdog cart to say 'thank you' because her Mothers back is completely healed and pain free. Gypsies kicked off as I prayed for her and her common law husband/partner.

174 Sikhs healed in town of stomach pain and back pain. A group of Sikh woman in their twenties with some children brought hotdogs, chatted, moved in healing etc. Thank you Lord.

175 Young lady returned to say that I prayed a weird prayer for her excruciating toothache, it went and never returned! It had kept her awake at night. She did not believe anything was going to happen. Her Nans toothache was healed too! She told me that her Nan had trouble with her back, so I prayed over a napkin for her to take with her.

August 11ᵗʰ 2008

176 Lady with husband sitting on a bench in the town centre. She had a metal crutch alongside her. The Lord said: "Go and ask her if she is in pain, then tell the pain to go in Jesus name". She was from Norway, and in pain due to a knee operation. I asked if I could say a few words, so the pain would leave. She said, "Yes as long as it did not cost her money" (they looked middle class). So I said: "Pain, in Jesus name, GO!" I went back to my hotdog cart and moved to Starbucks from WHSmith. Twenty minutes later she walked past me and said: "Thank you! All the pain has gone!"

August 14ᵗʰ 2008

177 An audacious Salvation Army lady called Mary in Portsmouth healed instantly of arthritic shoulder and arm. Had been asking God for the healing. Lady called Gloria also healed of arthritic thumbs.

August 15th 2008

178 In town today with hotdog cart. Lady on bench with two metal crutches. Tendon injury in hand, wrists and fingers. Pain and limited movement. Also no knee cap and one leg six inches shorter. Prayed for hand, pain left and movement in fingers. Prayed for her knee and leg. (Needs a miracle) Prayed for her daughter too, arthritic wrist etc.. Daughter felt the Holy Spirit touch her wrist (very smiley) Thank you Lord.

August 16th 2008

180 Two miracles today. In town with hotdog cart. A Sikh man on bench with wife. He had a crutch. His leg was severely damaged below the knee and to the side due to an accident. There was a lump and excruciating pain there and in his hip. I asked if I could pray. Yes. Placed hand on lump to side of knee and on his hip, prayed and the lump disappeared under my hand. The Sikh man was utterly amazed. I asked him to thank Jesus.

His wife then had prayer for her back. Heat etc. Immediately healed. Thank you Jesus. I was amazed too.

August 22nd 2008

181 On coach to Disneyland Paris, forty minutes from hotel. Lorry lost control on bend and crashed into the side of coach. Coach written off. God's grace, only some superficial injuries to people at the back of the coach. If lorry had collided a second earlier the coach would have been knocked over and into a ditch on the side of the road. Potentially horrific! "Angela Holidays." Thank you Lord.

August 31st 2008

182 Young woman with broken wrist brought hotdog. Temporary cast. Asked if I could pray for her? She said yes but was nervous in case it was a joke and I was going to make the pain worse. God took away all pain immediately when I prayed, she was amazed. Off she went with her father.

September 4th 2008

183 (see also 172 and 173) Nicole returned to say she is basically off heroin/crack. Also that her mums back has greatly improved. No sign of cancer in her body!!! YEE HAH

September 6ᵗʰ 2008

184 Baby Warren (Junior) and Mother. Caesarean operation, swollen stomach, pain. Brought a hotdog and had prayer on September 4ᵗʰ. Warrens Father came to me today to report that Warren and Mother are in excellent health.

September 7ᵗʰ 2008

185 Man returned today (Everest double glazing) to say thanks, due to a prophetic word, that the next three months would be of unusual favour. He told me that the day after he received a £18,000 order for double glazing and the day after that another order 'back to back' which is unheard of.

186 Hindu ladies son, all charges dropped!

September 12ᵗʰ 2008

187 Polish man Greg, karate man. Returned to say thanks. Severely broken ankle healed. Miracle. Surgeon could not understand how a 'new bone' joined 'the gap' where the ankle had been severely broken etc. His friend (atheist) now believes in God and Jesus after witnessing this. He was with him at time of prayer.

188 Woman in motorised scooter starting to walk, previously unable to do so due to no balance. Thank you Jesus. Amen.

189 Chappie (down and out) outside Above Bar Church with dog. Toothache etc, prayed. Love/compassion anointing. Pain went while praying for 3-5 minutes. Praise God.

September 17th 2008

190 Yesterday Bruce came to my hotdog cart to say that his Auntie had been healed. He did not believe it was God, but the medicine. Severe depression. After ten minutes he shared about prison, hard life, four brothers to look after, no best mate and that he wanted to be a healer. Shared Jesus.

September 20th 2008

191 Bonny returned to say the temporary cast had split in two. Her broken arm is completely healed and strong. Although she is meant to have the arm broken and reset next Friday, it is obvious that it will not be needed! The Lord has revealed himself a lot to Bonny.

192 Natalie returned to say he knees are healed. She looks after her disabled Dad. Prayed for her knees and a job for her. Thank you Lord.

September 21st 2008

193 Young University student with hay fever. Prayed for her by smacking the side of her head once in the name of Jesus. She returned one hour later to say that the hay fever had gone, and she was open to hear about God and Jesus. Amen.

Please note, one cannot go smacking people 'In the name of Jesus' as a formula, it has to be instructed by the Holy Spirit.

194 Man who moved into 'Olan Mills' photography, had bad knee due to skiing accident. He offered me a drink of coffee with him and his assistant. He told me about his knee, so I prayed, and I really sensed Gods healing flowing into his knee. God had broken out and due to that was able to talk to the man. The assistant lady had a faith in God which had been knocked back due to circumstances in her life whilst living in New Zealand. The lady told me later on that day that the knee had greatly improved. Praise God.

This healing was therefore not just beneficial for the man, but the assistant lady also as it would have helped to restore her faith in God.

195 Family looking for dog, Above Bar Church 'beggar', I asked if anyone needed healing. The man had injured his hip, a lot of pain. I served them with hotdogs, I took the man by his hand and was led by the Holy Spirit to pray by putting a hand on his shoulder too. Prayed. Knew God had touched him. Went back to serving hot dogs to his wife.

When he started to exclaim he was utterly and totally healed. Amen. Amazed he was! To the glory of Jesus. Amen.

November 3rd 2008

196 Bonny turned up to say her liver was 'all clear' after prayer where the Holy Spirit instructed me to slap her back/liver area twice.

197 Young man with girlfriend, broken arm from boxing a punch bag. Had support on his arm. He had been in pain for over a year with it, and limited movement. He took off the support and God healed his arm instantly. Amazed they were etc. Praise God

198 Lady Catholic friend (in her sixties), healed within ten minutes of chest infection/phlegm etc. Witnessed the previous miracle that prompted her to ask for prayer. Thank you Jesus.

199 Man came to say 'thanks' as his Daughter had made a full recovery of 'heart' problem. She was only given a 50/50 chance of survival. He was all emotional.

November 8th 2008

200 Well to do lady, (around sixty years) came back to say 'thank you' as her back was 'wonderful' after prayer. I pointed to Jesus, she said: "I now thank him every day." Hallelujah, that's what it is all about. Personal relationship with the Royal Commandment. Amen.

November 9th 2008

201 Abraham (Avy) pedlar returned into town today. Banned from peddling due to no work permit. His Sister was with him. She said her stomach was in pain. Was now better after prayer. She had asked me to pray three/four days earlier but confessed that she had not told me the real problem due to embarrassment. However, the Holy Spirit spoke to me via a word of knowledge, and a directional word of command/prayer. Speaking to her menstrual cycle and associated areas into correction/order and healing. Thank you Jesus/Elohim. Thank you.

November 12th 2008

202 Lady worker at G+Ts, Highcliffe healed of damaged tendon in ankle etc. In pain. She came to me five minutes later to say that it was healed. Praise God.

November 17th 2008

203 A young lady returned to say that her friend was healed of a 'wheat' allergy after prayer. (She was present when I prayed)

November 20th 2008

204 At work, walking to the loo, pass a small group of young men in their twenties. As I walked past, the hand of the Lord touched my spirit (head down) and I knew a certain man had a bad back. I prayed for him, initially the pain subsided, so I prayed a second time. My hand was shaking as the Holy Spirit flowed through me etc. He went on his way with his mates, five minutes later he came into Pret-A-Manger and shook my hand. Smiling cheek to cheek. Healed. Praise God.

November 23rd 2008

205 Unloading van of hotdogs, man in his fifties with daughter stopped to mention about Sainsburys having no hotdog rolls due to me. (Annoyed) The lady was on metal crutches due to a fused ankle and arthritis in lower back and leg. So offered to pray. Yes, prayed 'loose' and she then put her fused ankle on my foot because she did not want me to touch it. So prayed and to her astonishment she now had loads of movement in her 'fused' ankle. She said 'JESUS' in astonishment. The geezer said: "You can have as many hotdog rolls as you want, and I will never moan about it again!" Both had smiles on their faces, I asked them to thank Jesus and expect total recovery. Praise God. Thank you Jesus.

November 26th 2008

206 'Ellie', lady who works in the German Market; hurt her foot badly, on metal crutches. Off work weekend etc. Prayed over a napkin and asked her friend to get 'Ellie' to place napkin on foot. She was back to work within two days. No crutches completely healed. Thank you Lord.

November 27th 2008

207 Young lady, eighteen years, (friends with the lady who was healed of 'wheat allergy' (203) was also healed of stomach-pain she had for over a week. Amen, praise God.

November 28th 2008

208 Two miracles today, first a Scottish man with walking stick ad hotdog cart. Fused ankles and plate and pin etc. Prayed all pain went and lots of movement in ankle. Gobsmacked he was. Praise God!!

209 Lady healed ten minutes later. Sciatica and back pain due to compressed discs in lower back etc. Pain left and movement etc. Thank you Jesus.

December 2nd 2008

210 Down and out lady came for hotdog. Had sling on arm. Said her arm/shoulder was damaged and she had to have pins put into it as they could not cast it (shoulder area). So prayed, she 'claimed' total healing and full movement without pain. I would like to declare this miracle and await confirmation in case she was 'blagging' a free hotdog?

I've had opportunities to pray for quite a few people lately; and Gods hand has been with me.

December 5th 2008

211 Mother returned to buy hotdog and say 'thanks' as her small child was healed of 'colic' after I prayed by slapping her hand and asking her to put it on the girls tummy. The 'colic' was all gone in two days instead of weeks etc. The little girl of about two years was unsure of me because she did not like me slapping her Mums hand.

December 12th 2008

212 Lady with back brace (plastic) who was in pain due to broken back said all pain had left her after prayer.

213 Jamie who sold me a C.D duplicator; had a bad back for over a year. Said his back was completely healed after a twenty second prayer. Shocked he was, as he had been sharing about 'trans' meditation.

214 Mark (Steve's friend), said his sister in laws knee was completely better one hour after prayer

God has been good and is good.

January 3rd 2009

215 Down and outs eye hurt badly in gas explosion; with burns to ear etc. Prayed, sigh restored, eye ok. Ear healing nicely. Thank you Jesus.

216 Liverpool man (big issue) returned today to say he had 'all clear' from cancer tests. He had previously asked me to pray. I prayed in a loud rebuke and he was not pleased with that; however he is all clear and I instructed him to thank Jesus.

217 Disabled chap waiting to park next to my van as I was unloading etc. Ogle Street. As I put my hands onto the steering wheel to move the van the Lord showed me that he had a bad lower back. So I asked to pray for him after he joked about a zimmer frame to me. I put my hand in the exact spot where his vertebrae were fused. Prayed. He said he felt better, 'funny enough'. I then prayed for the woman with him who was suffering from insomnia. That was also a word of knowledge. She was gobsmacked. Thank you Lord.

January 10ᵗʰ 2009

218 A black nurse who attends Victory Gospel Church came to my hotdog cart today to report that E was now speaking. An amazing recovery as she was in the neurological ward in Millbrook due to two major aneurysms in her brain. Diagnosis was that she would be severely handicapped in recognition/speech. (Maria Claire went with me to pray) Thank you Jesus.

January 24ᵗʰ 2009

219 Woman with son brought hotdog and said her son was prayed for by me two years ago. He was suffering with asthma. Totally healed, no return in two years. Lungs healed. Amen. Thank you Lord!

220 A teenage couple stopped me as I was window shopping in town outside the jewellers. She requested I pray for her boyfriend as he had a constant pain in his jaw due to root problem. She knew that God had healed one of her friends arm through me previously. I explained that it was from God as I started to pray. I knew that God had already started to heal the root and jaw etc. The power and healing of the Holy Spirit hit his jaw like a shaft of light. I prayed with the knowledge of the manifestation of the Holy Spirit. Asked him to move his jaw. Completely healed. Praise God they asked. Amazing.

February 21st 2009

221 Muslim man returns to say thank you for healing to his back. No need for walking stick. Healed!

May 1st 2009

222 Prayed for woman in the PM meeting at Church. She had a broken foot in a temporary cast for at least five weeks. Had boot on etc. She felt the power of God heal the foot. During praise and worship she testified that it was healed and told me she could move her toes. It took courage for me to pray for her during praise and worship. I am pleased.

May 5th 2009

223 Woman that I had met last week came back again with her daughter. Bought a hotdog. She sat on bench with it. Her daughter (18-20 years) took her Mum the hotdog as she was sitting on the bench. I thought her mother shouted to her: 'Pray for my back' but she was really asking for a napkin. So I went across to her and asked: "Can I pray for your back?" She was gobsmacked and said yes. Then her daughter came over and asked me how did I know that her mum had a bad back? I then explained about God/Jesus. Ten minutes later I asked her to check her back out. Completely healed after six months of pain. Held her hand while I prayed. Thank you Lord. It was fun.

May 10th 2009

224 Family of five brought hotdogs outside W H Smith. Lady had pain in body and back. Started in hand. They were Christians. Prayed for her (loudly). Five minutes later the pain was gone, flexible back etc. Praise God.

225 Lady upset due to husband hospitalized. (Stress etc) Due to the praise and worship C.D, she found a heavy anointing of the Holy Spirit. Fell on her for around half an hour in the town centre, tears etc. So she told me, so we prayed, and she took a napkin etc.

226 Lady approached me with a similar experience of the Holy Spirit in town, listening to praise and worship C.D. She was a minister's wife. (Methodist Church in Weymouth) Her husband had been ill for five years; very hurt by people in their Church etc. She was overwhelmed by the Holy Spirit. So we prayed, and she also took a napkin.

227 'Gothic' girl healed of pain in back as I prayed by hotdog cart in Ogle Street around 5pm. Instant healing.

Thank you Lord!

228 Testimony at West End Church. Lady said that her daughter had now conceived after napkin prayer. Ha Ha Ha.

End of June 2009

SUPER GRACE! I've let slip keeping a written account of testimonies, however over the last two weeks there has been FOUR healings and miracles after prayer.

July 7th 2009

229 Yesterday I was in a pub playing pool. Two Irish travellers playing pool. J (18 years) and M (around 20 years) Brothers. J had about twenty stiches on one side of his arm and around the same on the other. He had pain in his arm due to the injury. He also had three metal plates in his arm. I prayed, all the pain went. I then prayed again and there was heat in his arm. I asked him to check for metal plates, they were no longer there. All you could feel was bone. Praise God. I talked about Jesus and they were acquainted with being born again. Although still travellers yet they did not swear. I prayed for M back due to a word of knowledge.

July 8th 2009

230 Prayed for middle aged lady with hand support at Flowers of Justice Church. After I prayed all the pain left her arthritic fingers and hand.

July 10th 2009

231 Prayed for a young woman in her twenties. She had half of her thumb missing due to an electrocution. Stump at top of thumb. No feeling in her thumb. Nerves dead. As I prayed for her in the pub by the pool table, the wonderful Holy Spirit said: "She is healed." I asked her if she was healed and she was very shocked and amazed. She asked me: "Who are you?" I pointed her to Jesus. She said she believed in Jesus. I then prayed for her boyfriend as he had a neck that cracked when it was moved.

October 1st 2009

232 Lady (63 years) was at Restoration Church, West End. She showed me some baby pictures of a boy called 'Toby', a miracle baby.

233 Two men returned to report healing from cancer:

A Scottish man from Winchester healed from lung cancer. He initially did not want me to pray. Totally healed. Very happy.

Organ player from Sholing. Had prostate cancer. Prayed loudly for him outside Central Hall after meeting. Went to Sholing to teach on glorious Church. He said he was healed, no cancer, prostate normal size and that he had to watch his weight. Also gave me a money gift of £100. Thank you Lord.

234 Two ladies healed in the photocopying shop, Hedge End. Heard her talking about her knee. In pain constantly due to knee operation. Went back to shop, prayed. Knee healed instantly. No pain, full movement. Her boss/owner also wanted prayer for a sore throat. She was afraid that it would go to her chest. Did a loud rebuke "GO" in Jesus name. She was startled and overwhelmed that the lump had left her throat. Praise God.

235 C and E, C was in considerable pain due to a fish sting whilst swimming in the Philippines. Stung on the side of face and neck. Was going to see a neurologist. Prayed. Anointing flowed. Healed by God as he testified a while later, it worked! I said: "Thank Jesus." He said that he already had! Ha Ha Ha!

236 Prayed for the town centre manager's girlfriend. After word of knowledge concerning her bad neck. Healed after rebuke in Jesus name. Thank you Jesus, thank you Lord.

October 9th 2009

237 In town, black youth aged 16-18 years. Temporary cast on hand due to broken knuckle. Prayed, healed etc. He was amazed! Very natural, very easy. Good God!

October 15th 2009

238 H, ex-boxer. 80 years old. Spiritualist for 40-50 years. Knew some of the 'great spiritualist healers' etc. Had injury to 5 discs in back due to an accident many years ago. Prayed, with discernment of spirit/Knowledge. Saw Holy Spirit pouring healing onto him, had words of knowledge regarding how he was being healed via Holy

Spirit. All pain left. Also prayed for his arthritic knees. He knew the lady in the photocopying. (see 234) Small world.

235 Elderly lady was also prayed for at the same time. Head aneurism and pain in body. Very open to being prayed for, especially as H (above healing) was so enthusiastic about sharing with her a bunch about healing etc. I have prayed for at least 5 spiritualists in the past two weeks!

236 Muslim man returned to say "Thank you" for healing his back two years previously. He has a Christian wife whom he loves. Was able to share with him God and Jesus etc.

November 16th 2009

237 Teenager about 19-20 years. Stitch marks on hand, he said that he had severely broken his hand and foot. I had prayed when he had a temporary cast on. Within one week his hand and foot completely healed! No permanent cast needed. It was a miracle. He has a check-up in six months' time. He returned to say thank you and to shake my hand! I pointed to Jesus.

November 18th 2009

238 Hayley said that a 'whole' family had become Christians and were attending Victory Gospel Church due to husband getting his back healed after prayer beside my hotdog cart. Thank you Lord.

November 20th 2009

239 Prayed for black man last week after word of knowledge concerning his bad back. He was in his twenties and quite big. Had an opera singer figure. He was a Catholic and was surprised and grateful that I prayed for him. He returned yesterday to say thank you, back healed. Praise God.

November 22nd 2009

240 A 15-17 year old teenager returned today to say that I prayed for his wrist that had been severely broken; after praying it healed quickly. The operation was not needed etc.

November 24th 2009

241 B sent me a text to say, 'Her knees are fine, she walked into Poole and back today.' I prayed for her knees after visiting William last night as it was his birthday. I prayed for B by my car as I left. Took my hand and she placed her foot on top of mine. I saw the healing fall on her via discernment of the spirit. Praise God. Thank you Jesus. Lord please become more real to B. Thank you.

November 29th 2009

242 Aster House, in the morning. With Bob Light. Marcus died, drug addict. His sister shared how I prayed for her mum in town three weeks ago. Bad knee that needed an operation. It kept her awake at night. The next day it was completely healed. Her doctor was amazed. (Then the sister and daughter received Jesus and Holy Spirit.) Her brother K also received instant healing to shoulder. He was a weight lifter and a Christian. Praise God.

December 4th 2009

243 Polish homeless man returned for a hotdog. He was ecstatic that his back and shoulder was better after prayer a couple of days earlier. Had an inclination/word of knowledge that he had a bad back. Due to the language barrier he was quite apprehensive about letting me pray for him. Praise God.

December 10th 2009

244 Shaun, Janine's son. Broken ankle at youth club. Was in temporary cast. Came into town centre on crutches. Prayed. God healed his ankle. No sign of fracture on X-rays. Gone, healed. Shaun was like a magnet in receiving healing. Praise God.

April 15th 2010

245 Lovely miracle today. Young lady about 18-20 years old. Indian Christian with two other Indian ladies around the same age. Bought a hotdog around 3-4pm. She had metal crutches. Had hurt her knee severely. Knees kept dislocating. Needed surgery. Had to be put in cast, then brace etc. Prayed. Within one hour she returned, carrying her crutches. Completely healed. Yahoo. Thank you Jesus.

June 21st 2010

246 In obedience to Ada's prophetic word to me a week ago:

"Not only will the insane and severely demonised be set completely free to be trophies of God's grace, they will also be empowered by Gods glory to glorify his name."

1 Corinthians V 27-31

Ada prophesised that God almighty would start to speak prophetically, and that it was time to write down the words he gives. P.s As I have such a memory to remember ha ha ha

August 27th 2010

There have been many notable healings and miracles beside the hotdog cart in the past 2-3 weeks. Many opportunities to pray for people. There has been the presence of a big Angel in front of me as I serve hotdogs. I have also sensed a small cloud in front of me. On a few

occasions I have sensed this Angel and the power of Gods persistence to heal has manifested alongside this Angel. Last night an orb of three colours: blue, white and pink was beside my head as I lay down to sleep. It was within an arm's length. Beauty in a bubble. It was not 'beauties', but 'beauty' itself. I was really tired, so I pulled some of this beauty into my face. My hands tingled slightly with the presence of God. I then went to sleep. On waking, I considered this orb. I believe it was some of the 'beauty of Gods holiness' in a bubble. A small quantity, a pin prick of Gods beauty contained in his holiness. Earthly things that 'look' beautiful are a mere reflection of true beauty. It is only an image of beauty, not beauty itself. What we describe as beauty is a tarnished image of the true beauty of God. The image of earth's beauty is incomparable to the heavenly and divine. Even the image of the earthly is in a fallen state due to sin and death. Real beauty has a substance to it. It is living, it does not look beautiful, it is beauty itself. Part of who God is or whatever he touches and breathes into is alive. Beauty lives. The beauty of Gods holiness.

November 11th 2010

247 Unloading hot dog cart, 11am. A depressed young man walked past, big issue seller. Really down he said. I prayed for him by hugging him tightly and releasing the life of God out of me and into him. He felt the anointing transfer into him and went his way. In the afternoon, approximately 3pm, he saw me in town, he looked and sounded like a completely different person. 'Vibrant' Romans 8 v2. Praise God. Thank you Lord.

November 17th 2010

248 At Dudley for a conference. Stayed at quality hotel. Prayed for chambermaid (around 40 years). Tennis elbow. Lots of pain for two weeks. Gentle prayer, anointing flow etc. Healed and noticed the difference immediately. Next day, prayed for her friend, head chambermaid. Prayed for her broken heart and over a napkin for her dad who had lung cancer. Told her to blow on her dad's chest in the name of Jesus and place napkin over him too.

November 22nd 2010

249 K had sciatica in her back. Prayed for her. Asked her to pray too, asking Jesus to heal her back. Instant healing. Praise God.

December 11th 2010

250 Sikh family came to buy two hotdogs, husband, wife and two children. He reminded me that I helped him in the summer at Homebase in Millbrook, I transported something to his house in my van. I prayed for his dads shoulder and it was completely healed. He returned six months later to say thank you. Thank you Jesus, amen.

251 A returned to say his face and smile were now recovered as I had prayed for him a week previous. He looked like he had been to the dentist. Praise God. I had also been led to pray for him during the week in regards to his ministry.

252 Someone returned to say that their aunt had been healed of a severe pain condition and no longer needed a stick. Three months ago I had prayed for her.

God please prepare me, emotionally, mentally, physically to carry your authority and anointing glory.

253 Two Scotsman say they are breaking free from heroin due to prayer.

254 Woman with fracture in foot. In a wheelchair next to my hotdog cart. As I was praying for her, she felt heat go into her foot. She requested prayer for rheumatoid arthritis, the presence of God was all over her, head to toe. Praise God expect a miracle.

255 Sikh family had an experience with God some time ago, heat, pain free.

December 14th 2010

256 A chap returned to say he had not had an alcoholic drink for 28 days since being prayed for. I prayed for him on Ogle Street corner. Hayley was there too. Praise God.

December 22nd 2010

257 A woman returned today to report a healing miracle to her in the summer. Hay fever, she was perplexed to how 'I did it'. I explained it was God via Jesus etc. She then asked me to pray for her husband who was sceptical. I said that I would pray anyway. He had problems with his shoulder and a disc in his back. I prayed, and the presence of the Holy Spirit was evident, very strong. I then prophesised over him in regards to the healing anointing on his hand (like a glove), and his calling in God to be an evangelist. He said that he was from Denmark and seemed overwhelmed by the whole experience. His wife was overjoyed and hugged me. She said: "We will see what happens!" Praise God.

January 2nd 2011

258 J (KFC) texted me to say that a friend of hers had been prayed for by my hotdog cart. Her 'lymphoma tumour' had disappeared, much to the amazement of her surgeon who was responsible for her operation. He was puzzled as to why she was there because her x-ray had come back completely clear, even though her previous x-ray showed a large tumour on her hip, where she had fallen and hurt it badly a year previously. Praise God!

January 4th 2011

259 A young woman in her early twenties was prayed for regarding fear, so I said: "In the name of Jesus", and blew on her as instructed by the Holy Spirit. When you pray for captivated people, 'blow on them' in Jesus name. She is now free.

January 7th 2011

260 At 'Secret Place' January conference. With Ada. Prayed for a lady that had difficulty walking, crutch, bad back, pain due to a broken back. Healed there and then. After prayer, also prayed away depression for her. Glowing she was. Good good good.

January 9th 2011

261 Praise God! Yesterday at meeting in praise and worship time with 7-8 others. I was in the spirit of praise and worship when suddenly I was aware of 4 or 5 'great ones' standing next to me to my left. It was such a surprise I said: "WOW", to be in the presence of such great people. Why did God allow me to experience this? I know that in heaven nobody will have to wear badges, crowns or clothing to show their 'reward of greatness'. For it will be part of who they are. It is part of their being. You see them, and you know that they are honoured by God as 'great ones'; everyone knows they are great. It is amazing to us earth folk!

262 After the session, an elderly lady asked me for prayer regarding stomach pain and sickness. She said a heat had penetrated into her stomach and stayed there for one hour. The sickness left her instantly and she was healed. Praise God.

January 14th 2011

263 In town today, heard a testimony concerning an alcoholic who I prayed for with a loud 'rebuke' in Jesus name. Has not touched a drop since. Thank you Jesus.

It's the anointing, thank you Lord.

February 15th 2011

264 Kaley, the one and only, said that her 'sciatica' down her leg had gone. Yippee.

265 Over the last two days, at least four people have approached me in town and requested 'healing prayer' out of the blue. Also, one chap had brought his mate for healing to his back because another one of his friends had received a healing to his back previous. It worked! Praise God, praise God and praise God!

February 16th 2011

266 Man (elderly) in a motorised scooter, returned to say thank you as his gangrene leg was totally healed after prayer about two weeks ago in the town centre. He was chuffed to bits.

267 Man returned today to say thank you as his foot healed rapidly and all pain had left after prayer of 'command'. He had been begging in the doorway of Above Bar Church. Chinese New Year it was, really good man, really pleased, praise God.

March 3rd 2011

267 B Maggie at Flowers of Justice Church Bassett had suffered from epileptic seizures for many years. After a loud prayer/command, all seizures stopped. The flickering sunlight through trees no longer affects her too. What a lovely testimony. Praise God.

March 3rd 2011

268 Chris from Above Bar Church rang me to say a chap (M) from south London had been instructed to find the hotdog man in Southampton, and that I would pray for him. Chris was unsure and apologetic etc. Little did Chris know, I had already spoke to M five minutes before. I had prayed to God earlier that day: "What do you want me to do today?" A prayer that I do not normally pray. I then met M, had testimony time, prayed and anointed him. I also gave him one of my scarves. God was in this big time!

March 12th 2011

268 B This elderly lady returned today in her wheelchair. She said: "She has not been able to walk for 45 yes... 45 years! As I prayed, a gift of faith was evident. The anointing power of God went down her neck to her spine, then to the bottom of her back. After some coaxing due to the cold weather, she took off her blanket off her legs and walked around the hot dog cart unaided. A miracle. She did not sit back in the chair. I encouraged her to carry on walking. Praise God. (Please read testimonies 101, 117, 124 & 268 – this is Jean the same lady received four miracles from God by the hotdog cart).

Jean had told me she had been paralysed for over 40 years. Her husband's name was John and I testify that I saw the back brace removed, I saw the neck brace removed, I saw the calliper on her leg removed and I saw the two lumps due to tendonitis, on her hand disappear instantly after prayer and I also saw her get out of the wheelchair unaided and walk round the hotdog cart twice. I witnessed all these miracles after prayer with Jean, with her husband John present; which God did, and I give Him all the glory. Also Jean had two daughters and she said one worked as a nurse at the hospital.

269 V came into town to pick up book and reported a couple on the bus said that they had a 'miracle baby' after prayer from the hotdog man. Thank you Jesus.

270 Young man's hand instantly healed on my way to van via Asda. He had broken his hand recently. He told me he was a Buddhist as I was praying, God healed him there and then, in Jesus name. Three girls also watched the miracle.

March 16th 2011

You are about to arise in resurrection power. Lord grant me your Holy Spirit of revelation, wisdom, might, power, knowledge, fear of the Lord and quick understanding. Grant me justice, righteousness and faithfulness. Thank you Lord. Amen.

March 20th 2011

271 Maggie (see 267), healed instantly of carpel tunnel in wrists at Flowers of Justice Church. Praise God.

March 22nd 2011

272 B reported that her stomach is healed after prayer round my mums. Acid gone, pain gone, vomiting gone. Noticeable anointing and 'gift of faith' to pray for B. Thank you Lord.

March 26th 2011

273 Was praying for someone by hotdog cart when I overheard a young woman say: "He healed my mother's hernia!" So, another testimony! Praise God and thank you Jesus.

March 27th 2011

274 At West End Restoration Church. The man's back was healed who I prayed for last week. He had commented how my hand had gone hot and cold when it was placed onto his back which proved to an analytical man that it was not my body heat. God spoke to him in a way that was profound to his thinking. Praise God.

The consequence of darkness is sickness/death. The consequence of the light is healing/life.

March 28th2011

275 Round Adas, phoned J, she said that all 'abnormalities' in the babe that she is carrying (due April 29th) have disappeared after prayer in January. Remarkable.

276 Lady known as Helen, although her name is 'Helena' bullied at school as children emphasized the 'a' at the end of her name. Around 33 years old, in a wheelchair for five years at least. Condition with spine, hollow bones like bamboo. God will supernaturally heal her, fire will pour down her back and she will be totally restored and be able to walk again.

April 25th 2011

277 Lad, 17 years old, said his brother had been healed of deafness. He had a hearing aid when I prayed for him around Christmas time. His brother had been deaf since birth. His brother is too embarrassed to see me as they all laughed when I prayed at Christmas. Praise God.

May 6th 2011

278 Lady was walking towards hotdog cart with support strap on wrist. I enquired about the pain, she said she was in "agonising pain for 11 weeks." Broken bone in hand etc. I asked to pray, she said "yes." I prayed, then asked her to check it out. Complete instant healing, no pain! Full movement, she took off support and did not put it back on. She carried on walking and returned with her husband to thank me. They were very grateful and enquired about healing for their grandson (13 years) as he has bad legs. Praise God.

279 Man named Robert, friend of Steven who was healed of cancer, returned to say his throat was totally healed, all the hoarseness was gone. His next check-up at hospital was in 6 months' time, doctors happy, as they were concerned it was cancer. Praise God.

May 8th 2011

280 Lady returned to say that her hand/wrist was completely healed, also her husband was walking much better as his knees were prayed for with a loud "GO" command.

281 Intense heat of Gods healing Holy Spirit on a man's leg where he had broken it, temp cast. He was a commercial fisherman and with his girlfriend/wife. I knew where the two breaks were in his leg 'before' praying for him. Thank you Lord.

May 9th 2011

282 Was at youth club tonight, did the God Slot, preached on Isaiah 53:5 and Mark 16. How the youth can pray for others. Afterwards, some of the youth prayed for each other, instant healings happened: Pain in back healed instantly, pain in foot healed instantly, knee pain healed instantly.

The 3 youths found it fun to pray for each other and were amazed at the instant answers. Praise God.

May 23rd 2011

283 I went to a great conference in the week with Heidi Baker and Ryan Wyatt. Worked Sunday, two instant healings today, a young man (18-20 years) was in a group, prayed for his injured ankle. Three weeks injured and in pain due to football. Instantly healed, it was a hand on shoulder prayer. HEALED. Put hand on his shoulder, and imparted anointing via a prayer as Holy Spirit showed me how to minister via a picture in my mind/spirit.

284 Also a severally depressed woman healed after a hand on shoulder prayer. I had to reassure her before praying as she enquired as to why I was praying for the sick and initially did not want public prayer. After sharing my testimony about how God healed my lungs many years ago and showing Gods Love, she had prayer and her face literally lit up. She said she felt all woozy, (how the tranquillizers made her feel etc.) Praise God. In the spirit

I had seen white doves flying in the air above Southampton before praying.

May 24th 2011

285 Prayed for a pedlar from Senegal, his wife was seriously ill with fever in hospital in Spain. Gripped with a high fever, so I prayed there and then with the man present. Took authority over fever and commanded it to GO. Prayed at 2 pm, at 3:45pm the man from Senegal had tears in his eyes as he reported he had a phone call to say his wife was now completely healed and discharged from hospital. The fever suddenly and immediately left, as the prayer took place in Southampton. Immediately. Praise God.

286 A Big Issue seller asked me to pray for his knee, he could not bend for three days. Prayed, hands on knee, then told him to bend his knee. As he bent the knee, it was instantly and completely healed. The prayer was a loud LOOSE in Jesus Name. Yahoo! Thank you Lord.

May 29th 2011

287 Yesterday I approached a Lady by the leading of Holy Spirit. She had fibromyalgia and was in constant pain. I prayed for her, blew on her 3 times, instantly no pain. Her husband was astonished.

288 Heavenly Father thank you. A chap (around 20 years) limped up to buy a hot dog. Very painful blister on heel of foot due to ice skating, Asked him to place his foot on top of mine, prayed, instant healing and pain went immediately. Ha ha ha!

June 3rd 2011

289 A man I prayed for with an injured arm/elbow at the exit to Blacks, with N observing, exclaimed to N that his arm was instantly healed and had full movement after prayer, where previously it was stiff, and locked. I had gone straight after prayer to get my van.

290 Heard that a man named John S had the most amazing miracle when a cloud and light entered his hospital room. I was in same hospital seriously ill, at age of 30 years old when this occurred. He was now reading his bible openly at work, where previously he had been a foul mouthed atheist with an aggressive temper who hated God and Christians. That's 18 years ago. Praise God, what a testimony. (Much more to this than the short paraphrase.)

June 15th-25th 2011

291 Arrested in town after loud music and prophetic declaration and preaching. The message was:

"God wants his babies back." God is going to visit the Satanist/dark magic/Witchcraft people, and those followers of Satan will have personal encounters with God, they will see "who He really is," that will cause the lies/deception to be broken of their minds, and 'many' will follow Jesus and become 'Great Witnesses.' Saul to Pauls. That fire would come out of the dragon to destroy but would return to destroy the dragon.

Within 1 week of the prophetic preach, a young man named M who had been initiated into 'Satanism' at the age of 10 years old, met me with a young man from

126

Poland. His request was to receive the Holy Spirit. I have only witnessed a few people who literally Light up like a light bulb when Receiving Holy Spirit, M is one of those. A first fruit of what's to come.

June 26th 2011

292 Round a Sikh friend's house. Prayed for J, she had a cyst in her ovary. Loud Rebuke in Jesus Name, it dispersed immediately. As a spiritual person she also felt it leave. The loud Rebuke is very effective when of The Holy Spirits instruction, leading etc. Thank You Jesus, amen.

293 A man's back instantly set free after a Loud Release in Jesus Name command. Very tangible anointing. Love, Mercy, Thank you Lord. Out of my belly will flow the breaking forth of many waters.

July 2nd 2011

294 Went to meeting at CCC. Roland Baker was ministering, the next day I prayed for woman with carpal tunnel syndrome in both wrists, prayed, instantly

HEALED, and took straps off. Then prayed for Lady with support strap on one wrist, had not been able to bend wrist for a year, HEALED instantly.

295 Young lady on metal crutches told by doctor she had 4 more weeks on crutches. Very bad knee, so I asked to pray for her. Laid hands on knee, lots of heat, she was startled as all pain left and she was able to walk without the need for crutches. Praise God.

I was not feeling like praying for anyone today, yet I did, and God answered, Amazing.

July 14th 2011

296 Young man with arm in sling sitting with two young woman outside W H Smiths. I asked him what was wrong with his arm. He said he had broken the upper arm two days ago and they could not put it into a cast. He said he was in considerable pain. I prayed, laid my hand gently on upper arm, asked him to make a fist with his hand. INSTANTLY HEALED,

PRAISE GOD.

July 16th 2011

297 Elderly man returned to testify with his wife from South Africa that his knee was completely healed. I had prayed for him a few days ago and the power of God was present to heal. Praise God.

July 20th 2011

298 A couple of days ago, I was unloading my hotdog cart and some scaffolders were working near Blacks camping shop. There were two of them. I felt lead to give them a hotdog, which they gratefully received. God gave me a word of knowledge for the Irish/Newcastle man regarding his back, I knew instantly where the pain was and that he has weakened his back in an accident. I prayed for him, placed my hand in the exact area of pain. The Holy Spirit anointing of Healing was ministering to the area. Praise God, later he told me he had fallen 110 feet and resulted in an injured back which caused him ongoing pain. Isn't God WONDERFUL?

August 5th 2011

299 A Polish Man was on the way to the Dentist to have all his teeth removed, he stopped to say that the doctors were 'amazed' at the recovery to his knee and leg after prayer. I prayed for his teeth and jaw, yes you guessed correctly, the dentist did not need to remove any of his teeth.

August 6th 2011

Get ready for Miracles, signs and wonders says The Lord God Almighty, for they (Gods enemies) will be muted, dumb founded, and dumb struck. The Miracles, signs wonders are a testament to Gods Mercy and Grace, and evidence of the Resurrection of Jesus His Son.

You are about to Arise in Resurrection Power, Great Power = Obedience to God.

300 A Sikh lady brought relative for healing. In BHS restaurant, I had a word of knowledge about arthritic knee, prayed, lots of heat went into knee. Instantly healed. The other Sikh lady felt the healing go into her back, eyes and knees. (Isn't that a song?!) Praise God forever & forever, Thank you Jesus.

301 Prayed for a young woman at the Saints vs Leeds match outside the King Arthur pub. Her lower back has improved. Praise God, thank you Jesus LORD.

August 24th 2011

302 Peter (Lens mate), helped me move my hotdog cart into town as my van was being repaired. Praise God. I prayed for his arthritic elbow, and the Holy Spirit Fire went into it. The Lord spoke into my ear and said: "He only wants a partial healing as he wants to claim disability next year." To his astonishment, God healed him completely. He is still healed 6 years later and tells people that he was the biggest sceptic regarding God. Thank you Jesus.

303 Prayed for elderly deaf lady today, who could hear clearly with hearing aids after prayer. Also prayed for her hips, as she needed a Zimmer frame. Had been watching videos of healings in Chile by Dr Steve Ryder. I laughed with joy and excitement and expectation as I prayed with her.

304 Very quiet in town today. At 12:30pm, God had me prophecy to Jamie the statue man that it would be packed with people at 1:30pm when it was still empty. Within one hour the town centre was packed with people.

August 25th 2011

305 A lady and young daughter (5-6 years), returned today to say THANK YOU as her husband was having a nervous breakdown. A napkin was prayed over and put under his pillow. She returned to testify a remarkable 100% complete recovery and turnaround. Praise God.

306 Russian car wash man reported his wrist was completely healed after prayer yesterday, strained wrist it was. Thank you Jesus.

Today the Lord spoke into my Spirit in a very gentle voice and said you are surrounded by Satanists. Prior to this a young woman went into a 2 minute tirade of swearing and profanity in a very loud voice at someone she did not like. Very foul mouthed she was.

I then perceived a man outside Starbucks continuously muttering under his breathe, I was led to put on the C-D song "Oh how He Loves us," as this song played so the Holy Spirit of might and power rested on me. I then loudly proclaimed God's Love for the people of Southampton. The Satanist manifested, he could not stay in the Presence of God's Love that had replaced the place of profanity and hatred previously released into the atmosphere by a tirade of foul mouth swearing. As Gods Heaven and Light dissipated the darkness, the man jumped up out of his seat, and left very quickly. As he went past me I proclaimed Jesus Loves the Southampton people, to which he did an obscene gesture behind his back out of public view. I then noticed at least 4 adults wearing satanic pentagrams around their necks at the West Quay entrance. They had surrounded me exactly as God had said. Never experienced this again in such a public way. God is good, and a canopy of God's Love and protection covered Southampton for that bank holiday.

August 28th 2011

307 Praise God. A well-educated man who helps out at Central hall reported a remarkable healing to his back and hip after 10 years of pain. Plus his foot also miraculously turned into its correct position. I had prayed for him approximately two months previously.

There has been a considerable number of healings of lately. I have forgotten some of them as they were not recorded, however some people may return with confirmations.

September 1st 2011

308 A chap returned with his fiancée and baby daughter to say that the doctors were amazed at the recovery/healing to his lower leg after prayer by Starbucks. He said his leg got really hot as I placed my hand there and prayed. THANK YOU JESUS.

309 Mother and daughter bought a hot dog at 5pm today near a shop named Butterflies. She remarked her foot was hurting her, there and then, so I asked her to put her foot on top of mine, prayed. I knew God had instantly healed her. She was totally amazed that the pain had gone immediately. Praise God.

September 24th 2011

310 Met D (Lens friend), she thanked me for praying for her as she was given three months to live. Six years later she is very well. I will not go into detail however it is an amazing testimony.

October 1st 2011

311 Young man returned to say thank you, he had a temp cast on a fractured wrist. Was meant to have a permanent cast put on. Was in pain and prayed for. Instantly healed. Returned to hospital, no permanent cast needed. Thank you, thank you Jesus.

December 2nd 2011

Lord said let the journal restart...

312 Two young men in their early twenties returned to testify, they wore 'Tapout' shirts and were boxers /cage fighters. In March of this year I had prayed for one of them with an injured knee. Not only was the healing remarkable but he was equally pleased as he knocked out his next opponent with that knee, the knee that had been dramatically healed. I asked for his hand, and we said a prayer of Thanksgiving to JESUS, YES .... YAHOO!

December 7th 2011

313 Jamie (statue man) elbow broken, prayed. Next morning when he woke up, he took a shower, suddenly he was completely shocked and overwhelmed to realise he was using the arm and elbow he had broken only a couple of days previously. He was so shocked a few swear words were uttered. He was sharing this miracle with people he met for weeks afterwards. Of course this is medically impossible, so people smiled, and did not make eye contact. Joke.

314 German market trader, German sausage lady, extensive cancer throughout her body. Visible on side of nose, looked horrible. Prayed twice, the third time asked her if there was any noticeable improvement, to which I noticed the cancer was absent from her nose, & brand new skin was there.

December 15th 2011

315 Maggie, mother of Naomi, Flower of Justice. Testified of healing to heart and epilepsy, after prayer for epilepsy she had a fit that night, and never since. That was over a year ago. She has wonderful faith, hears God, and a gift of Dreams. Praise God, thank you Jesus.

February 9th 2012

316 Just went down to Botley shops. Saw a group of 5 youths (18 - 20 years) four lads, one girl. As I approached them, the Lord said one of them has a bad injured shoulder, right hand side. So I said: "Good evening, which one of you has a bad shoulder?" Ben said: "I have, right side." So he let me pray for his shoulder, even though he was anxious. I prayed twice, on the second prayer I held his wrist, and to his surprise it went really hot. The young Muslim man then asked me to pray for him, as he had torn a muscle in his arm, when in a fight earlier. I placed my hand on the damaged arm muscle, and casually talked to the group. After approximately one minute, I removed my hand and his muscle was completely better, no pain, full movement. He then asked me to pray for his eye that was stinging due to a fight. I blew on his eye, prayed, instant healing. I was then able to pray for reconciliation for Ben's family.

317 Laundry lady Anne at Swathling told me that her daughter had the all clear, epilepsy no more, shadow on brain disappeared, no trace of it on scan even though it was certainly there before Christmas. Prayed for her in a form of a prayer cloth. Miracle. Thank you JESUS.

February 14th 2012

318 Polish man homeless, set upon by some men from Birmingham, severally damaged his ankle. God had me pray for him two weeks ago, this Sunday his foot is completely healed. Miracle.

319 Polish man in town, prayed for his back two days ago, healed. It took some time and kindness via hotdogs to form a trust, so he could receive a prayer. God revealed himself by answering that request and showing His Love to him. Thank you Lord.

320 A man named Burt saw me today in town, said his foot had a miracle, the metal plates had been removed. I prayed again, and his foot was still hot 20 mins later.

March 3rd 2012

321 Another man returned today to say Thank you, he had an eye infection. His eye had swelled to the size of a golf ball, prayed, next day on waking up, his eye was completely healed. No swelling, no pain. Thank you Jesus.

March 6th 2012

322 Miracle explosion in town centre today by hotdog cart. Especially broken bones and injuries to bones. Wrist healed instantly. Elbow healed instantly. Hand healed instantly, and some others too. Praise God. God says a season of miracles in Southampton, also up and down the country. Praise God.

March 17th 2012

It appears that God is really pleased with me, it is as though he is showing off in the way His Love, and Power are manifested through me. Praise God, I am shining with Gods Light, people keep asking where I have been on holiday/sunbathing. On the 14th March, God said to me that I am going to cause you to shine (literally). Also the healings and miracles are continuous, every day... it's amazing and I am so excited about what God is doing. Especially 'through' me. Thank you, thank you and thank you. I have a thankful heart and give him ALL THE GLORY.

323 I saw myself very briefly in the Spirit. My spirit-man was all fire, my inner man was ALL fire. I noticed this but did not give it much thought. Plus my hands get heated up at times, especially fingers. Yesterday I prayed for a man with an ankle injury. I placed my hand on his right shoulder. Lightening went through his shoulder into his ankle, I saw this happen in the spirit, the man felt lightening and electricity go through his right shoulder and into his damaged ankle. His left ankle became hot, exactly where the injury was. It was all so very real, as I saw it in the Spirit.

Toby and Aimee came to me at lunchtime for prayer for family reconciliation, put my hand on their shoulder, and their shoulder got hot. Interesting?

March 18th 2012

324 Kerry healed of cancer, being mentored in her new faith by local pastor. Amazing Grace.

325 Young Italian woman bought hotdog from me. She was in a group of about twenty language students. The woman was on crutches with a strapped up ankle. She sat on a bench with some of her friends eating her hotdog. I approached her to ask if I could pray for a healing for her ankle. She said she was a Christian and that she believed. I took one of her crutches, placed it on her ankle and prayed. The next day, I met a group of the students who exclaimed with excitement their friend was "completely healed" and no longer needed crutches or physiotherapy. Praise God.

326 Young woman from Poland instantly healed of pain and stiffness in knee after surgery. Instantly healed. A man from Redeemed Church was giving out invites at the time, he witnessed an instant answer to prayer on the streets. Thank you Jesus, who is Lord.

March 21st 2012

327 Man (30-40 years) returned to say his leg was prayed for 2 weeks ago, that he felt heat, and tingling in his toes. His toes were in a permanent curled position due to an accident to his leg and nerve damage. His toes are now straight, and he can wiggle them. All pain has gone from his leg. I then prayed for his damaged knee, as he wanted prayer for that too.

328 (see also 325) Young Italian language student returned in person, to confirm healing, 100% healed, mobile and very happy.

329 Sylvia said acid reflux has gone after prayer.

330 Many instant healings today. Lady sat on a bench near hotdog cart. Two metal crutches. I went over and spoke to her, off work for six months due to ligament damage to knee. In considerable pain, untouchable. I knew The Lord was going to do an instant miracle. After permission I placed my fingers very gently either side of knee and prayed. Instant miracle. The woman was in a state of shock, when I asked her to move her knee, the knee moved fluently without any pain whatsoever.

April 7th 2012

331 Woman from Above Bar Church with fuzzy wuzzy bear hair. Had temp cast on wrist due to break one day previous. Instantly healed. She also testified to police on duty.

332 Lady on a cruise ship "Balmoral" from Texas, USA. Significant improvement to her back after prayer.

333 Kim's mum brought someone to me for prayer, breast cancer, also named Kim.

334 A traffic warden who has had constant headaches for months and had to wear dark glasses as a result, returned today to say thank you as all headaches stopped immediately after prayer.

335 Prayed for the tyre man. It was quite humorous as I had a word of knowledge for a bad back. There was an overweight large man working for him, so I presumed it was him. However it was the thin tyre man! He was in so much pain the he could only sleep upright on the sofa. Prayed and he felt the Power of God heal his back. Praise God.

336 Prayed for two Southampton Football Club reserve players. The player with the injured back I prophesied to. I told him that he would play for England as a full international in the future and that he would become an England captain too. I think he was a defender. Also prayed for his colleague who had a slight knee strain.

April 15th 2012

THANK YOU LORD... 11am approximately... Revelation substance from Heaven poured all over me. Tangible spiritual substance poured down over me like a waterfall. Unsure how this will manifest, but it surely will.

April 18th 2012

God did not only want us to feed the poor, and the homeless. He wants us to really show them His love, to REALLY LOVE THEM.

337 Travelled to Poole Quay to pray for Julie, Matt's sister. Arthritic hips and legs, on crutches. Prayed. Fifteen minutes later she was off the crutches, pain almost gone. Weeks later still healed. Ironic as I was meant to pray for another Julie in Poole with cancer.

May 20th 2012

338 Indian lady returned to report her broken wrist in a temporary cast had healed rapidly after prayer. She did not need a perm cast. Praise God.

May 21st 2012

339 Lady returned to say that her gall bladder was completely healed after prayer. Pain left immediately, and condition was cured.

May 24th 2012

340 In Millbrook estate. Went to my car, there were approximately twenty youths by the shop entrance. The Lord said one of them has a bad foot. I looked at the group, went to the car, got something out, looked again and saw metal crutch being waved in air. I walked up to youth with metal crutch and asked him why he had the metal crutch. He said that it was his friend's crutch, and that his friend had chipped a bone in his big toe. In front of ten youths

I asked him (14-15 years) if I could pray for his big toe. Yes I could, so I did that by placing my finger on his shoe on top of big toe. I shared about Heaven being a real place, stars, day time etc. I then asked the lad to check his toe, to his "utter amazement" it was totally healed and pain free. I asked him to thank Jesus, then went for my cup of tea.

June 1st 2012

341 I noticed a man with a bad back stand near my hotdog cart, I asked him if he had a bad back. He replied yes due to a gastric illness, which he had suffered from for two years. He was in "constant pain" that affected his back. The doctors could not diagnose what it was. I Bound the 'spirit of infirmity' in Jesus Name, and commanded it to RELEASE the body. INSTANTLY healed after two years of constant pain. Full movement, pain gone, the man was astonished. Two Christians came along and shared Jesus with him. Perfect timing.

June 4th 2012

342 A black lady who had a knee and ankle injury for a year. In constant pain. Was healed instantly after a hand on shoulder prayer as instructed by Holy Spirit. Praise God Forever.

343 Her Lady friend was also healed instantly. She literally felt the bone move in her lower back and all the pain left. She was 'Gobsmacked.' Both were already believers with much faith.

344 Lady with wrist strap on healed instantly, plus her hip was also healed instantly after prayer.

June 22nd 2012

The Holy Spirit said, "I want you to go to the next level," at which I doubled over as The Presence of God 'touched me' gently. Going to the next level in the things of God is in connection to walking in the Spirit, going from Glory to Glory, entering into a place in God that is new to that individual. The Old Testament type of The Promised land is a New Testament spiritual experience of knowing Gods Glory. Being mentored by The Holy Spirit to walk in and experience that realm of Gods Glory. This ultimately comes out of a place of relationship and revelation from God.

July 1st 2012

345 Tom returned to report that the cancer has gone from his stomach. He was prayed for two months ago, he said doctors are amazed.

July 9th 2012

346 Mark and his one legged brother turned up for a hotdog with a male friend, a hard looking man. He complained that he had pain in his stomach for years, as a result of pancreatitis. He allowed me to pray for him. The anointing of my BEAUTIFUL GOD touched his stomach and he felt a 'warm glow' and all the pain left.

July 14th 2012

347 Man returned to say thank you as all scans are clear in respect to his stomach.

348 A few returned to say thank you regarding answers to prayer, especially getting jobs. Thank you Lord.

349 A lad who had injured his knee was prayed or in front of his friends who were well amused. Next morning when he woke up he was amazed as his knee was completely healed.

350 Broken arm in temp cast, prayed, rapidly healed, 'next day' went to hospital. Cast removed. Miracle.

August 3rd 2012

351 Two broken bones in feet healed 'instantly' in town centre this week. One was a gothic lad who was part of a group who hung out with the people who hold advertising signs for tattoo shops. He was totally astonished. Praise God.

August 8th 2012

352 Marian returned to say that she had been healed of 'cerebral palsy'. She was still in a wheel chair and requested prayer for vertigo and cartilages in her knees. I felt lots of heat on knees and rebuked vertigo loudly. Praise God.

August 16th 2012

353 YAHOOO. Young lady returned to say that 'all the epileptic fits' had STOPPED, after prayer. Thank You Lord.

I then had a word about her boyfriend (20 years) about nightmares he was suffering from. God spoke into his future. Praise God, Praise God.

August 21st 2012

354 A 20-30 year old woman returned to say her finger broken in two places no longer needed splints after the fire of God healed her rapidly. Praise God.

August 23rd 2012

355 Ulcerated colitis woman returned with an eagle t-shirt from Virginia USA. She had been dramatically healed after 18 months of pain in her stomach, all healed, all pain gone. She did not believe in God and did not expect to get healed. Neither did her husband. Praise God.

August 25th 2012

356 The Lord did a demonstration of instant healing today at 5pm in town today, amongst a group of army personnel. One groin was healed instantly of all pain as I blew in Jesus Name. (Gift of Faith) Word of knowledge as

God healed a man by heat touching his left side, others in the group also had pain leave instantly.

September 20th 2012

357 A Christian lady who I knew said that her blood pressure was completely back to normal, after years of high blood pressure. The doctor said to her that there was no medical explanation why this should happen and happen it did.

September 27th 2012

358 Brian returned to say that a chap named Karl who was prayed for by Andrew White and myself, did not need a back brace, as his vertebrates were healed. Brian said he has now started attending church after years of back sliding.

October 6th 2012

359 Yesterday God healed a broken shoulder instantly, the young man broke it three days previously. He had a sling on and was told it would take eight weeks to heal. Praise God.

October 7th 2012

The Lord says, "Cancers will come to you. God will smash them to smithereens and heal those people. It's time to execute judgements on the wicked, and on behalf of Gods Kingdom, 'judge' yourself, so you can 'judge' sin and evil."

360 A persons back was healed after prayer. Sciatica faded, lungs cleared of obstruction and excess phlegm cleared from breathing. Full lung capacity restored. By faith I pulled two new lungs out of heaven.

361 Young man with tumour on the brain, with a fund raiser for cancer care. As I prayed, the man's head heated up, his face went redder and redder and redder which is a good indicator. God said I want to burn the tumour out of his head with Holy Spirit FIRE. Praise God.

October 8th 2012

362 Young lad around twelve years who I prayed for about three weeks ago returned, he had suffered severe psoriasis for years. Scabby head, eye brows etc. On returning, the psoriasis had disappeared completely. No sign it had existed. This prayer was administered through an act of blowing this psoriasis away without touching him, thus signifying The Holy Spirits work.

October 12th 2012

363 Lady with crutch by Starbucks commented on my music. I asked her what was wrong, she replied that she had Lupus. She was in pain all over her body, no feeling in feet etc. so I asked permission to pray for her. Yes. Put hands on ankles. 'Release in Jesus Name.' Then placed hands on shoulders, back and head. Then God showed me healing being poured all over her. She was amazed at the heat all over her body. I instructed her to thank Jesus. Five minutes later she returned in floods of tears and a state of joy as all the pain had gone. I then prayed that she too would heal the sick via Jesus.

October 17th 2012

364 Darren who had been on crutches for seven years due to ankle injury. He had damaged nerves and no feeling in his feet and toes. Instantly healed today, it took three seconds of prayer. Charlie and gypsy the dog were eye witnesses. Charlie said about the loss of disability payments.

October 25th 2012

365 Achilles' tendon. The Holy Spirit instructed me to demonstrate a miracle publicly as Burt placed his foot on bench. As I prayed, the tendon literally moved twice, which Burt felt happen. Instantly healed. Bob was a witness. Praise God.

October 31st 2012

366 Halloween in Calshot, selling hot dogs at a street party. Managed to pray for three ladies. Arthritic hand, back and carpal tunnel. Word of knowledge. The women were astonished by the heat administered to their affected areas. I was pleased as these ladies celebrating Halloween seemed quite spiritual.

November 21st 2012

367 A man who had his curled toes straighten out after a prayer, brought his friend for prayer. It was in pain and had problems with its knee. He was sceptical however the next day there was vast improvement. I said Jesus wants you 100% healed as he died 100% so the price is paid for you to have 100% healing, not 90% or 80 %. NO. 100% healing, and we should not settle for anything less.

November 22nd 2012

368 Finished work early as there was horrendous weather. Had a word of knowledge for a traveller man in van, prayed for his hip, instantly healed. That was the word of knowledge, "Pain in left hip." Instantly healed.

December 16th 2012

369 I was serving a man and a woman with a hotdog and had a word of knowledge that the woman needed prayer for healing, so I asked her. Yes she did, she had 'Crohns disease.' So I prayed for her, The Lord instructed me to rebuke the disease loudly, so I informed the lady I would raise my voice and God would strike the disease like 'lightening.' I animated a bolt of lightning strike the disease and shattering it. God manifested healing, my hands got hot and she felt the presence of fire. They thanked me and went on their way. Within one minute a bolt of lightning flashed across the sky and thunder sounded. What an unexpected sign. There was no other thunder or lightening that day, the thunder lasted three minutes and there was only one flash of lightening. I will take that as a sign/wonder. Thank you Lord.

The sweet wrapper covers the sweet and looks nice, but it is not the sweet. As so the body of a person is wrapped around the spirit and soul.

January 17th 2013

370 Really awful weather and low foot fall. About 4pm a tangible anointing fell on me. A man came up with his hand in a permanent cast, he had broken multiple bones in his wrist and hand. I prayed for him after a word of knowledge, that God would move his bones back into place. I did not auto suggest anything. As I prayed, he was startled as he felt the bones move by themselves in his injured hand. Amazing

371 Then three men came up for hotdogs. I had a word of knowledge about bad necks etc. All three of them had neck problems, one had previously broken his neck and had ongoing pain, the second had trapped nerves in his neck and the third had whip lash from the dodgems at the funfair.

All three had prayer, the first felt tremendous heat on the affect area where he had previously broken his neck, the second felt heat on his neck without hands being laid on him and the victim of whiplash received a release prayer all within ten minutes of each other. Bang bang bang. 'Dunamis' power, thank you Lord.

372 Also that day, I prayed for a woman on crutches who needed a pioneering cartilage operation, so I reached into Heaven, got new cartilage and placed them into her knees. I then said three days. The boyfriend said, "I hope it works!" I replied, "three days, no hope about it." The spirit of doubt and unbelief was trying to steal the rhema of God from the ladies knee. That's why Smith Wigglesworth was so adamant and strong about not moving Gods Rhema word when ministering to the sick and needy. He knew Gods word would be tenacious in the good fight of faith. He is honoured as an Apostle of Faith.

February 3rd 2013

373 Young man and woman around 18 years came to purchase a hotdog. He had an arm sling on. Dislocated his shoulder three days previous. Was told that it would take around two months to heal. He reluctantly allowed me to pray. The healing came down my left side and God said that he is healed. I did not believe that it would be so quick and easy. This had not happened for a while and doubt was present for an instant miracle. He moved his shoulder and was in shock and amazement as it was all OK. Praise God.

374 Two days ago a homeless British man had pain in his jaw and teeth. Looked swollen. Prayed for him, big smile, healed! He walked past today, and he told me that he was so happy he could eat nuts again as they were his favourite.

February 4th 2013

375 Indian man who broke his elbow and hurt his back due to a fall. He was in considerable pain and wanted to be prayed for. Miracle to elbow within five seconds of prayer. Then I proceeded to pray for his back. Thank you Jesus, healed. Really good.

February 15th 2013

376 Beautiful, wonderful, fantastic, brilliant, amazing, great! A simple man talked with me yesterday beside my hotdog cart. His right pupil was three times bigger than his left pupil in his eye. He had damaged his eye as a child and had partial sight in his right eye due to this. So I prayed, and his vision improved dramatically. I was amazed that he was so cool about it. I thought he was just trying to be nice, but after a simple eye test consisting of me pointing out different signs in the street, it was clear that his eyesight had improved. I asked him to tell his vicar where he went to Church!

March 1st 2013

377 Three people that I did not want to pray for were healed today as I laid hands on them. Two gypsy ladies who sell heather in town both had pains in their backs. Looked really painful. Big smiles on their faces as I prayed, and they received their healing. Very receiving they were!

Also, a man with a broken collar bone was in pain and had his arm in a sling. Prayed very casually for him. Asked him if he felt anything. "Oh yes" he replied. He felt heat on his collar bone as I had my hand on his elbow as instructed by God. Pain left, movement restored.

This just goes to show that the spirit is willing, but the flesh is weak. Our ways are lower/earthly, but Gods ways are high high high.

March 3rd 2013

378 Word of knowledge about a soldiers foot. A company of fellow soldiers watched as he placed his foot on top of my foot. Prayed. Healed instantly. Praise God. Also, one of the rookies said "believe" as he had witnessed this previously a few months ago.

379 Indian friend that was studying media. Prayed for her, immense fire fell on her, she was startled! Prayer for 'sweet sleep.' The Lord also healed her period cycles. Great testimony of Jesus Christ.

March 14th 2013

380 Lady in her early twenties returned to say 'Thank you' for the healing of her fractured elbow in the summer. Rapid healing after prayer. She was going to send her child to church.

381 Tom's lady friend said that 'Frank' was healed of cancer to the throat and chest.

March 17th 2013

I am overwhelmed by how many people have returned in the last week or so to say 'thank you' for their healing. Probably around six people which is quite unusual but very encouraging.

381 Yesterday, a nurse came to say 'thank you' as he fractured ankle had healed rapidly and needed very little physiotherapy, which really spoke to her.

382 A young polish lady who had walked into a coffee table with a serious leg injury was prayed for behind 'Blacks.' During this, a woman manifested in her car and started to beep her horn and shout at us. Anyway, she had the cast on for two months, she was meant to have it on for a further two months. Within two weeks she was completely healed.

March 27th 2013

383 A mechanic who fixed my car light after an accident complained of sciatica in his back. I prayed for him indoors. Within one hour of being prayed for her was healed. In the afternoon he jumped over the neighbour's fence. He and his son passed me in town today and I heard his son say, "Isn't that the man who prayed for your back?" Yes! Praise God it was!

April 4th 2013

384 A young man said that his asthma had gone completely after prayer.

385 A man in his thirties came for prayer. All pain left immediately after years of agony in his back and hips. He wept as I prayed. He said that his friend had also been healed previously. Praise God. God showed me how to pray for him, so I simply followed what I saw and heard.

April 15th 2013

386 Lady with painful feet and pain in shoulders. Healed.

387 Man had been in pain after being kicked in the back. Healed.

388 Word of knowledge for a man with voices in his head. Thankful he was, I prayed discretely for him in his ear. Praise God.

April 30th 2013

389 Indian man delighted outside of West Quay, healed instantly of carpal tunnel diagnosed by the doctor. He was on very strong painkillers. Awaiting an operation to both of his arms. He received well. Praise God.

September 23rd 2013

390 A young lad about 14 years was with a group of around ten teenagers beside the walkway of 'Blacks' in Southampton. He had unusual grey coloured eyes. He told me that he had an eye condition from birth that affected the colour. I asked God for a miracle and then asked the lad to think of what colour eyes he would like. Two weeks later he has no disease and his eyes are the colour he asked God for. Miracle, sign and wonder.

391 Sikh man returned to thank me for his healing to his knees, he said that they were 99% there. I said, "Thank you Jesus, we want 100%!" and I blew on his knees. It took a lot for this man to thank me publicly.

392 A builder working in Primark was in his van outside, he looked tired with his head on the steering wheel. God said to me to say the word 'Peach' to him. So I did. He seemed startled and happy that I said that as a king of blessing! About a week later I saw him again, he told me that as soon as I had said the word, all the depression left him. His eyes looked really bright. Praise God.

October 29th 2013

393 A lady and her friend saw me today to report a miracle of healing to her son for a hearing defect. He had this since birth. Hospital said that it was a miracle. Completely healed. Praise God.

October 30th 2013

394 Man with painful foot for five years completely healed.

395 Rugby player, torn tendon in shoulder. Had six weeks of recovery still to go. Instantly healed. He was shocked. Yippee!

November 2nd 2013

396 Prayed for a black lady in town centre, outside West Quay. She had a bad ankle and a crutch for support. She was with a sister in Christ. I asked her what the matter was. Asked her to put her foot on top of mine. Prayed. Then I placed my hand above the ankle and prayed again. To her amazement, all pain had left, and she smiled. She walked away without the crutch. Praise God.

397 The gypsy lady whose dog had a miracle brought her friend into town today for prayer and healing. Her friend had cancer of the breast with a bandage over it where a quarter had been removed. They had also taken bone scans to see how far the cells had spread. Praise God for a miracle.

November 12th 2013

398 'Big Ian', the Victory Gospel minibus driver, and his wife returned today to say that his knee was healed. Also his wife's back.

399 Newcastle man who sleeps rough returned to say that his hand was completely healed after years of pain due to nerve damage from an operation on his shoulder. Full movement restored to his hand, no pain. Praise God.

November 15th 2013

400 Young man in his late teens came through town today with a temporary cast over his hand. He had broken his knuckle and needed a permanent cast. As I prayed with my hand underneath his, I heard "It is done." I asked him how his hand was as he said previously it hurt to touch his knuckles etc. To his astonishment, all pain had gone, and he had full movement. My prayer was no longer than ten seconds long. A man then came along and

167

through his negative words, tried to steal the healing. I rebuked immediately in Jesus name. Praise God.

November 16th 2013

401 John, Jeans husband, asked me to pray for his ears. He is deaf and has to use hearing aids. As soon as I commanded the deaf spirit to leave from his ears, he started to hear with his hearing aids out. I prayed again, heat was manifesting, and his hearing kept improving. Praise God.

402 Homeless man returned to say his eyes were healed. They were previously cloudy. I blew on his eyes yesterday. He now has clear vision.

November 23rd 2013

403 Word of knowledge via fire in my hand beside hotdog cart. Three teenage girls were walking past, I asked them if they had any pain. One said yes, in my side. She put her hand there indicating where it was. I prayed over a napkin and asked her to put it there in front of her two friends. Within three seconds the pain left.

December 12th 2013

404 As I walked past the big security guy on the entrance to the German Christmas beer tent, I was given a word of knowledge. I asked the chap if he had a bad back. "How did you know?" He replied. I said, "Can I pray for you?" "Yes." He said. I was directed to pray for the pain in his lower back and also his neck. God removed all of the pain instantly. The neck was a rugby injury from the past. About twenty minutes later, his colleague asked me what I had done to his friend. He then asked me to pray for him! He had a cartilage injury in his knee and was in pain. Praise God, he took all the pain away. Even one hour later he was pain free and enjoying bending his knee.

December 14th 2013

405 'Big Ian' from Victory (see 398) returned with his son. He shared an amazing testimony from about a year ago. I was meant to have had a word of knowledge about his son having cancer. I prayed for him and he is completely healed. I do not remember this at all. I found out that it was testicular cancer. He was told that he would never be able to have children, his partner is now pregnant. Praise God.

406 Mans broken ankle healed instantly. He still had thirteen weeks to go as they had made a mistake with the temporary cast. Prayed, heard the Holy Spirit say that 'it is done' and it was.

December 16th 2013

407 Went up to Hayes, Middlesex with Peter Poland, to buy a Mercedes. As we viewed the car, an elderly Hindu man came out to explain about his car with his daughter in law. He started to explain about his poor health. How he had a heart attack, lost weight and his appetite. After going into the house for a cup of tea and to pay for the car, the opportunity came to ask if the elderly man would like prayer. He said yes. I prayed for the gentleman by placing my hand on his stomach. I prophesised healing and health specifically into his heart and stomach. The manifestation of Gods healing love and power increased over a period of ten minutes. The room got hotter and hotter, without any heating to cause this to happen. The man's wife also had her knee prayed for with a loud rebuke as instructed for by the Holy Spirit. Immediate healing and heat into the knee which amazed her. "How did you do that?" She asked. She then phoned up the neighbour next door to 'get healing' for their enlarged and leaking heart valve. I blew on him etc. Returned to Southampton. I was really intrigued with how hot the room got in that house as God manifested himself. Praise God. Thank you.

December 24th 2013

408 A man in his fifties returned today to see me, he did work with Romanian orphans. He had broken his ankle severely. Was prayed for. I said, "Because of his mercy, God would show him mercy." The pain left immediately when prayed for. Today he said the hospital could not believe the x-ray of the foot as it was a 'supernatural recovery.' Normally a fracture of this type would need a minimum of thirteen weeks healing. The man had a boot on, no pain and was very happy. Praise God, I knew it by the Holy Spirit. He said that he would return again.

January 17th 2014

409 Bob, eighty nine years, reported that his grandson's brain tumour has vanished after we prayed in agreement in the high street around six weeks ago. Praise God.

January 27th 2014

410 A young teenager within a group of around seven young men came to buy a hot dog. I shared about a miracle, deaf lad, deaf since birth. Then I noticed that one of the lads had a bandaged hand. He had broken his hand and needed a permanent cast once the swelling had gone down. He allowed me to pray. I commanded the bones to knit rapidly. He could feel heat. When he tested his hand he was in complete shock as he could literally tap the area where the break was without any pain. There is no way he could do this with an unhealed break. Miracle.

January 28th 2014

411 A young lady called Emily who works for the Southampton Echo newspaper came to ask the question of the day and to take a photo etc. It was to be about 'Valentine's Day.' Anyway, the Lord intervened, and she was quite overwhelmed as she willingly received prayer for 'emotional' problems. The Lord gave me the words from heaven specifically for her. Destroying the lies of the devil. That is what the anointing does, it destroys the yokes of Satan. She was free and the joy she felt was electric. Hope, value and worth took the place of despair, worthlessness and hopelessness. Amazing to watch and be a part of. Thank you Lord.

February 19th 2014

412 Fantastic, my hand kept getting hot all day with fire. An Indian lady with a friend came along and asked her if she was in pain. She said yes, I placed my hand on her shoulder and prayed. Anointing fell and an hour later her friend gave me a Starbucks tea and cake as a gift of honour and respect for her friends healing. Praise God.

March 9th 2014

In praise and worship on my bed in Malta; when suddenly I recalled praying for a woman dying of cancer in

173

the U.K who died. Within this I remembered her two sons. They both had pay-outs due to their mother's death. I considered if the mother desired healing or whether she was happy to die as her sons would be well provided for. Anyway, as I wept over her death, (as I really warmed to her) I cried quietly. Suddenly lightening went into both my upraised hands and I felt in my spirit an impartation for cancer to be healed.

March 10th 2014

413 In a shop in Malta, healing to man with pain in his shoulder. Instant healing, no pain, free movement.

414 Elderly woman healed of pain due to calcium build up in the top of her neck and spine. Scottish lady on holiday in Malta with her husband who wore war medals.

415 Went into Valletta, two healings happened after speaking with a street trader from Macedonia. Fifty year old Maltese man was instantly healed of back pain and bent down to pick up a flower from the floor. Lady with pain in stomach healed.

April 1st 2014

416 Sat by hotdog cart, two Sikh ladies were instantly healed of osteoporosis in the back. Elderly lady was a quiet prayer, the daughter was a loud 'rebuke'. Both were amazed and emotional. Praise God.

417 Female canvasser in the Marlands shopping centre. Hand had previously been bandaged. She had cut it by a smashed glass door. Tendons were torn and needed stiches. Anyway, prayed for her with a Christian next to me. Movement started in her finger, then full movement. Was surprised. Lots of heat etc.

April 30th 2014

418 Sikhs healed in London. Arthritic knees and hip. Three ladies plus twins. Prophetic word for a baron lady. Also prayed for stage four cancer of the liver, lungs and kidney. Thank you Jesus.

August 30th 2014

419 Elderly lady with granddaughter. Asked if I could pray for her arthritic hands. The Lord instantly healed her hands with the Holy Spirit fire. Amazing.

420 A man who had a drink and drug addiction received prayer for pain in his ankles and feet. He was prayed for three times and received a miracle as he had suffered pain for twenty years. All pain left plus full movement in his ankles and feet. He showed me his left leg, a big chunk was missing above the ankle due to surgery. Thank you Lord.

September 1st 2014

421 A group of around ten Sikh woman with children came up to me in town by the hotdog cart. A lady was presented to me with arthritic hands. She requested prayer and looked slightly apprehensive. I took her hands in my hands and asked her to ask Jesus to heal her. She shouted a prayer, then commented that my hands were getting hot. I replied, "That's your healing." The fire of God touched her hands, I sensed that she was healed. I asked her to check her hands. Instant healing. She was startled, amazed and very happy. The other Sikh ladies were all happy about their friends healing and her surprised reaction. They knew that she would be healed there and then. Amen.

422 Young man with curly hair who sometimes stands with the statue man (street performer). He complained of pain in his foot and hip. Plays football. Prayed for hip and foot. Foot healed quickly. Saw him the next day, he said that his hip had got worse. 'Rebuked' infirmity in Jesus name, next day he was completely healed. Saw him three days later, big smiles and no more pain.

September 4th 2014

423 A most amazing day, business was awful for everyone and then suddenly there was the most 'extraordinary' anointing of fire. Within one hour, three people were instantly healed and touched with the fire of God.

Wayne, E-cigarette seller said that his fiancé wanted a 'blessing' for their baby. She would arrive into town just after 4pm. Prior to her arrival, I felt heat/presence on my left side, plus I knew that my hands were anointed. That's where the fun began!

A Jewish couple in their early sixties walked past my hotdog cart. After a brief informal chat, I received a word of knowledge for the lady. Problem with back. Prayed 'to' the almighty, placed hand on back, anointing fell etc. I encouraged them, off they went. Twenty minutes later, they returned. The man said, "You have fixed her back!" I replied, "No, not me, the almighty." I also referred to the everlasting covenants, Abraham, Moses, David. Israel was now formed forever.

424 Then a woman of around fifty years came out of Starbucks. She said that she was a Christian. I noticed she had a gold cross around her neck. She told me that she was having difficulty breathing. Asthmatic fear in chest. She felt like she had a heavy weight on her. Her third eye was open and affecting her at night (seeing demons etc.) She also had pain under her rib. Very concerned about it. Prayed for her, the beautiful presence of God came down. She felt the awesome presence of love and peace. All the heaviness lifted off of her chest. I sensed to shout 'FIRE', which I did, all the pain instantly left the rib. She lit up. She then prayed and asked God to 'close up' her third eye. God showed me that this was now closed. She would have good sleep, peace and shalom into her body, mind and soul. She left smiling and grateful. Praise God.

425 I then prayed for Wayne's fiancé, Robin. Prayed for a baby. She had previously miscarried, I spoke life into her. As instructed by the Holy Spirit, I placed my hands on her shoulders. She said that she felt heat in her stomach. I said, "Why in the stomach when my hands are on your shoulders?" I then prophesised about God using her to heal others in the future via Jesus. Her hands got very hot as I showed her the sign of the message. I also taught her about giving God back 'all the glory' and I told her that the next person she prayed for would be healed as a sign to her that the words were true.

426 Then a group of people came to the hotdog cart. A tall young man had a heart condition and a young lady in her late teens had suffered with pain in her knees for three years. I asked if I could pray for her first, she said yes. I simply said, "Thank you Jesus." The fire touched her knees. Within one minute she was completely healed. No pain and full movement restored. The reason I prayed for her first was because God wanted to show the young man his friend's knees healed to receive his healing. I prayed for him and a lovely heat went all down his chest. Increased as we prayed. The fire of God answering his prayer. Pretty amazing.

September 8th 2014

427 Lady called Sue from North Baddesly, purchased a whirlpool dishwasher from her. Prayed for her arthritic shoulder. Returned the next day to buy a fridge freezer. She said that he shoulder was healed, and she asked me to pray for her elbow. Irish Dave was with me. God also healed her elbow. Sue asked questions about God. One hour and twenty minutes later I left, and she said that she wanted to go to Church.

September 9th 2014

428 Returning from my mothers, myself and my son picked up a hitch hiker called Michael from Hythe. He had a back brace on and told me that he had metal rods in his back due to falling off of a roof. Prayed for him and the pain left.

429 Picked up two wardrobes and a double bed in Nursling. People were downsizing. Lady named Gemma was suffering from headaches. There and then I prayed for her. 'Blew' into her head. Pain left immediately, I knew this by the Holy Spirit. She was amazed.

September 12th 2014

430 Picked up a car from Winton. Broke down at Einsbury Park. Breakdown recovery to my mums. Got the bus back to Winton. Had a specific word of knowledge for a teen girl on the bus. She was with a group of friends sat in front of me. The word for her said that she was suffering repeated headaches. In three days they would stop. This would be a sign that God and Jesus are real. Her friend also said that she suffered from headaches. I knew that this was due to too much fizzy drink and not enough water. I asked her if I could pray for her. She said yes. So I asked her to say 'Jesus' and blew on her head from six foot away. She said that it did not work, yet one minute later she was totally startled that all the pain left. As I got off of the bus, I heard her telling a friend on the phone what had just happened. Also one of their friends said that she knew me from Southampton as she lived there. Amazing. Praise God.

431 Got indoors from the bus journey. Peter, my son had pain in his back. I prayed for him. 'Rebuke' hands on back, then peace. Blew on his back and his head. Pain left instantly.

September 13th 2014

432 Ladies broken foot instantly healed. She had an operation two days previous. I put my hand on the cast on her foot. Knew that the pain had gone. Praise God.

September 15th 2014

433 In city centre, a young woman around seventeen years who had severed her arm badly. She had a big scar across her arm and was wearing a plastic support. She had nerve damage and could not grip. In pain and was told it would take two years to heal. Prayed with her. God instantly healed her. She repeated a prayer asking God to heal. Miracle. She even rubbed the area of scar damage. No pain. Amazing.

434 Two Sikh woman approached me and requested prayer. One in her fifties and another in her early twenties. The younger woman was pregnant. She asked for a prayer for her husband to get a visa. As I prayed, her hand got hot, so I asked her to put it on her friends left knee, which had pain. Instantly healed. I was led by the Holy Spirit to prophesy that the baby would have a miracle ministry.

September 20th 2014

435 With my hotdog cart at Ringwood carnival. Prayed for a lady with a bad neck. She was told to come to me to have prayer by another pedlar who sold E cigarettes. After prayer all the pain went away. Her face lit up and she had a big smile on her face.

September 24th 2014

436 Two homeless people came to ask for some free hot dogs. One was in tremendous pain with a very swollen knee. After prayer, all the pain left. The man was gobsmacked. The man who was with him had a healing in his leg a few years previous. Praise God.

437 Two women were near my hotdog cart, one had a support on her arthritic thumb. She looked very serious. I enquired about her thumb. The woman was reluctant to let me pray for her, so I prayed for her friend to pray for her thumb. In doing so, her friend's knee was instantly healed. Tremendous heat went down her back as I placed my hand on her left shoulder. Then the reluctant woman's thumb was healed. All pain left. They both said 'thank you' to Jesus. Hallelujah.

September 25th 2014

438 Walking past the Bargate by Costa coffee. There was a group of young men sitting there. They said, "Oh that's the hotdog man!" So I went towards them hoping to minister. I sensed the Lord say 'ankle'. So I asked if there was anyone in the group with a bad ankle. Behold, one of them had an injury from playing football. Praise God. I put my hand on his ankle, lots of heat, healed.

439 Spoke with two teenagers, prayed for the girls mum as she had a slipped disc. Prayed by faith that by Sunday afternoon she would be healed. Then I prayed for the second girl as she had neck pain. Placed my hand on her shoulder, heat went down her back, healing her pelvis and bringing it into line. The Lord told me that it was due to a gymnastic accident. Healed.

440 I worked on until 6:30pm today. Met a group of Polish men. One had an operation on his back two days previous. Showed me the stitches in his back. He was signed off work for six weeks and was in a lot of pain. God healed his back, once again. Great manifestation of heat and fire from the Holy Spirit. Lots of rejoicing. Amazing.

September 30th 2014

441 Debbie came up to me in town today to say that a chap I prayed for seven months ago who was an alcoholic and given one month to live is now totally free of alcohol and doing really well. Praise God.

October 18th 2014

442 Prayed for a man two weeks ago with an ingrown toenail. In lots of pain, swollen. Prayed for him by putting his foot on my foot. Spoke in the name of Jesus to the toenail, commanded it to go back to how it should be. Came in today and it was completely healed. Opened him up to the gospel and knowing more about Jesus. His friend was also with him had the exact same thing, so I prayed with him and all the pain left.

October 20th 2014

443 PC Steve told me that PC Chris was amazed his back was healed, no pain after we said that we would pray for him.

444 Beverly's sister had a cancer disappear instantly from her neck this afternoon. No pain and full movement. She can now swallow properly. She was given until Christmas to live. She was on liquid morphine and had two McMillan nurses looking after her.

445 Two young woman beside West Quay entrance. They both worked in West Quay. I spoke to them and encouraged them as I had noticed that one of them always smiles and appreciates my music. I asked them if they needed prayer. One of them was full of flu and the other had just recovered from flu. The Lord had graced me with faith and I knew it was with me. I prayed for the first young woman with the flu and congestion. I put my hand on her head, the anointing poured on top of her and within seconds she was completely healed. She was amazed and happy. I then prayed for her friend, she asked the Lord to strengthen her immune system. I placed my hands on her shoulders, the fire came onto her and the heat increased to which she was gobsmacked. Jesus was glorified. Praise God.

446 Went to Titchfield carnival, great atmosphere. Met the gypsy sister of Heather who I knew from Southampton. She allowed me to pray for her two relatives who both had neck pain. I prayed for them by placing my hands on both of their necks. Instantly healed to their amazement and my delight. It was right there in the open, and they were open to receive. I was really happy. Thank you Lord.

October 27th 2014

447 A man and a woman came in today to say thank you for his partners healing to her back. He then asked if I could pray for his knee as he had ligament damage. I laid my hand on his knee and asked him to pray. After two minutes he said that his knee was white hot. Healed. Praise God.

October 30th 2014

448 Working late with the Hotdog cart and light up windmills in town. At around 7pm, a man named Abdul talked with me. I prayed for an injury in his wrist due to the gym. God healed him. Then he asked me to pray for his chest. He had pain there for years. I received some words of knowledge, prayed with him for around five minutes. Abdul then asked Jesus into his heart. I prayed for peace to fill where the evil spirits of infirmity had left. I prophesised that he would sleep well. Thank you Lord.

November 10ᵗʰ 2014

449 Young lady on heroin with really bad teeth came for a free hotdog. She said that she was in pain and looked like she was. I prayed, the power went through me like a surge of electricity. I then knew she was healed from the pain. The Holy Spirit had told me that she had been in pain for six months. I confirmed this by asking her afterwards. Thank you Lord.

450 Last night at Wokingham fireworks. A young woman recognised me from Southampton. She had studied there at the university. Fashion design. She told me that I always cheered her up with my music. Word of knowledge of the Lord for her, "Work in January is for three years, then she would be catapulted into the next phase of her life."

November 23ʳᵈ 2014

451 An elderly man returned to purchase a hotdog and say thank you for healing his severe arthritis in his body. All he would say was 'thank you' continuously.

November 26th 2014

452 The car wash manager was healed instantly of knee pain he had for over one month. He was amazed. 'Loose in Jesus name' healing flow, pain gone. I told him that Jesus is real! Praise God.

December 12th 2014

453 Man with pancreatitis in his stomach, digestive system was in a bad way and he had trouble going to the toilet. After prayer all pain left immediately, and his stomach and digestive system has been functioning as it should be.

454 Man selling toasties on the Christmas market, had arthritis in his hips and shoulders for four years. Fire of God went through his body during prayer, all the arthritis has gone, completely free and in no pain. Praise God.

December 21st 2014

455 A lovely lady returned to share how she was suffering from really bad back pain whilst pregnant. After prayer, all pain left immediately and never returned. Her partner also had a serious knee problem which is still healed to this day, so much he can carry her upstairs! Her vicar from Minstead has been greatly encouraged by her testimonies which is fantastic. Hallelujah.

456 Went to get some market trader clips from a young man working for the E cigarette man. He told me how his shoulder was in pain due to a boxing injury years ago. His shoulder would dislocate, and he would be in a lot of pain. I asked if I could pray for him, yes. The Lord said to speak 'strength' loudly into his shoulder and command the pain to go, which I did. I heard the Holy Spirit say, "It's gone." To his amazement, all pain had gone. Full movement in his shoulder. He was freaked out, especially as he had been an atheist. Praise God.

457 A man walked past my hotdog cart with his partner. His face on his left hand side was badly scarred. My heart went out to him, so I stopped him and asked him if he had any pain or nerve damage. He said yes. I asked if I could pray for him. He said yes. All pain left, he seemed shocked. His partner was smiling like a Cheshire cat, cheek to cheek. Amen.

December 20th 2014

I heard the Lord say to me: "Greater miracles are coming."

February 11th 2015 (confirmed healings from the conference held on 17th January)

458 At the Canterbury conference, God flowed powerfully through a woman called Sasha, a paramedic nurse with words of knowledge. I prayed for a young man who had an allergy to water. Only about thirty people in the world have this allergy. If water touched his skin, he would have a reaction of burning and itching. After prayer, he was completely healed.

459 A young man's hip was healed, his muscle was torn away from the hip, causing pain when he ran and when pressure was applied to that area. He was not expecting to pass his army medical the next week. He was completely healed and came second in the mile run for his army medical. Amazing.

February 18th 2015

460 Tony was completely deaf in his left ear due to an eight hour operation where they took three bones out of his ear to remove mastoiditis. Damaged eardrum. Prayed for him and some of his hearing was restored. Tested by clicking my fingers and seeing if he could hear. Thank you Jesus.

March 1st 2015

461 Chap came into town from London to pick up a coat. Was asking me directions for a nice place to have a drink. We got talking and he told me that his wife was sick, so I prayed over a napkin for him to take back home. He went off then came back, he said that he was brought up catholic and believes in Jesus, he says that he feels the presence of God and calls it spiritual as he does not realise what it is. I then shared a testimony with him about Tony (healing 460) and his deaf ear being healed. He was stunned and shocked because his name was also Tony and he had a deaf ear too! So I prayed for him and he regained hearing in his ear. He became quite emotional and left because he did not want to start crying in the street. I rejoice in what the Lord has done.

March 7th 2015

462 Today a young girl came up to order a hotdog with her friend. She asked for just the hotdog with no roll because she had a sore mouth. So I asked her what was wrong with her mouth. She said that she had an operation the day before on her mouth for a cleft palette. There were stitches all in the roof of her mouth. She was in pain. I asked her if I could say a prayer for her for all the pain to be taken away. She said yes. Said the prayer with my hands in the air then I asked her to close her eyes. I then gently blew on her face. Asked her to check her mouth. All the pain left, and she could eat the hotdog with no pain. The doctors told her that it would take her seven days until she could eat normal food.

March 21st 2015

463 Phil lost a quarter of his leg due to an accident thirty years ago. He had suffered with severe pain due to nerve damage. Tried lots of different medication that did not work. Prayed for him about seven months ago. He returned today to testify that ever since that day he has felt no more pain. He can still recall the energy he felt go through him. Told him thank Jesus. Praise God.

April 4th 2015

464 Indian Sikh woman in her twenties, she was with her mother and a friend. Told me that she had blurry vison and headaches for around two months. She had been to hospital for tests and had spinal fluid taken out of her back to investigate. Before I prayed, I had a word of knowledge come to me saying: "As you lay hands on her you are going to heal her." Instantly healed. After the prayer she said that her eyes were completely clear, all the headaches had gone, and she felt light. Total restoration. Told her to come back and tell me what the doctors say to her. Her mother then shared a testimony about how one of their relatives received healing prayer after being on crutches for months. Afterwards his knees were perfectly ok and to this day he never needed them again.

465 Fifteen minutes later, a man and daughter came and asked for prayer. He had arthritic knees and hands. His thumbs were especially bad. He had already had one knee operation that was unsuccessful, still needed another one for new kneecaps. After prayer he was healed instantly, all pain had left, very emotional. I also prayed for his daughter, she has a disabled son. Thank you Lord, I give you all the glory, honour and praise.

April 23rd 2015

466 Julie had been having nightmares since she was a child. She had been to a number of counsellors and they did not help. Returned today to tell me that her nightmares had gone because of the prayer a week ago. Thank you Jesus.

June 13th 2015

467 Acer, returned to tell me that after a simple prayer, his hay fever allergy had been cured. He gave all thanks to Jesus.

May 1ˢᵗ 2015

468 Man came up to get a hotdog with his carer. He was very unsteady on his feet due to deep vein thrombosis. Just came out of hospital the day before. I asked if I could pray for him. All the pain left from his legs and he had full movement restored. Prior to this miracle I felt the Lord touch me. There was a man and a woman waiting whilst this man was getting healed that saw this. I had a word of knowledge for the lady about sleep and fear. Prayed with her. Thank you Lord.

May 15ᵗʰ 2015

469 A lady called Carla was with her friend in town, came up to me. Had a word of knowledge about her back problem. Asked if I could pray for her. She said yes. Placed my hand on the exact spot where the pain was. Healed after six months of agony. Praise God.

June 22ⁿᵈ 2015

470 Lady returned with her baby who had a problem with multiple holes in heart. The baby had to go for an operation, but the lady asked for prayer on a number of occasions beforehand. The surgeons opened the baby up and discovered that the majority of the holes had healed. What was meant to be a major operation turned into a minor one. The baby is now two years old, very happy and healthy.

471 Man from Victory Gospel Church asked for prayer as he was told that he had fluid on the brain. Waiting for the results to come back from the scan that he had. I believe that he is healed.

August 8th 2015

472 A ladies dog named Clive got ran over by a polish man, she took him to the vets. The vet said the dog would never walk again due to broken pelvis. They wanted £260 to put the dog down. She took the dog home because she couldn't afford it. After hearing this, I prayed on a tissue, the lady took it with her and put it on the dog's hips and legs every day. She came back today to tell me that six weeks have now passed, and he is now walking. The vet said that he never witnessed anything in his life and was convinced that she took a different dog to him. Praise God.

August 9ᵗʰ 2015

473 Muslim man that works in Poundland came up to me today. Suffered with sciatica in his back for six weeks. Prayed with him and all pain has left. He can now touch his toes. As I was praying he said that he could feel vibrations in his legs. Thank you Jesus.

474 Andrew returned today to buy three hotdogs and to tell me that since the prayer we said together his life has been turned around. Asked him to thank God.

August 10ᵗʰ 2015

475 Tony who worked for Specsavers was prayed for this morning as he had a common cold. Since the prayer he has had no trouble with his running nose. He thanked the 'humble man' named Jesus.

476 Wendy returned to confirm healing on her broken finger after prayer. Thank you Jesus.

477 Word of knowledge for a woman with three discs gone in the top of back. After prayer all pain has gone, and the vertebrae straightened back into the right position. She asked how I knew about her back problem, I explained to her that Jesus told me because he loves you very much. She seemed to be in a state of shock afterwards.

478 A homeless man named James got burnt last night by somebody using a cigarette lighter, whilst he was sleeping. After prayer a warm feeling came onto him, he got so hot he started to sweat. Waiting to see the outcome of the burn. Bad back also healed. Praise God.

479 Woman with shoulder problem, she was in lots of pain. Pins and needles in her hands and she would wake up in the night with pain. Was given pain killers by the doctor but they did not help. I laid my hand on her shoulder with a simple prayer. Instant healing. Thank you to Jesus.

August 14th 2015

480 Miranda, had toothache, got her to put her hands onto her mouth and I blew on her. Pain left instantly. She believes in God and Jesus and talks to him all the time. Amen.

481 Man came past my hotdog cart and stopped to testify that his wife had been healed completely of back pain after prayer. No more pain.

August 15th 2015

482 Prayed for a man named Robbie two days ago as he was complaining of a bad chest, sore throat and pain in neck that he had been suffering with for around a week. I put my hand on his chest and throat. He felt heat come onto him. All symptoms have disappeared.

December 6th 2015

483 Young man came back to say thank you to me because he was told by the hospital that his foot would have to be amputated because of a serious accident. He reported that after a prayer at my hotdog cart, his foot has had an amazing recovery and there was no need for amputation. I give God all the glory, honour and praise.

March 6th 2017

484 Woman named L came up to me in town today accusing me of speaking cancer over her mum. I told her that I could not recall doing that. My friend Gordon who was with me at the time defended me also. The Holy Spirit then spoke to me via word of knowledge for L, God had seen her crying by herself. I shared this with her and the anger left her, and I managed to pray for her. Also prayed over a napkin to take to her mum. Praise God. Amazing how things can be turned around.

March 19th 2017

485 Man named Danny was involved in a serious car accident where he nearly lost his leg. He came to me around three months ago in his wheelchair. I was lead to pray for him. The doctors said that he was part of 5% of people with a special blood vessel in his leg where the surgical procedures were less complicated. He said he would never play roller hockey again and would walk with a limp. Today he is now walking completely fine and he told me that he played hockey for the first time last weekend where he was the top point scorer for his team. Thank you to the wonderful name of Jesus.

486 A lady came up to me and was attracted to the anointing. Asked her if she needed prayer. She said that she had problems with her pelvic bones and she had to go to the chiropractor regularly to have them fixed. Asked her if I could pray for her. She said that yes and she believed in a higher power. Prayed to align the pelvic bones and laid hands on her. Also sensed that she had a trapped nerve, so I commanded it to 'loose' loudly. I knew that God had done something. After I prayed for her she then replied, "I have studied psychology." I said "Yes, but psychology does not make or cause bones to move back into their correct positions. Did the bones move?" She said yes. She then left, I don't think that she wanted to hang around to talk. Due to the prayer and the Holy Spirit power, God had given something to that lady that she cannot put down to psychology.

Praise God. Hallelujah.

April 1st 2017

487 Went to pick up a Vax hoover in Poole. The lady who I brought it off said that she was selling it due to arthritis in her hands. She could no longer use it and it was too heavy for her. The dog also barked to it. Asked if I could pray for her. Anointing fell. After prayer all the joints were loosened, and pain left. She was wearing a tracksuit with hearts all over it. Talked to her about the love of Jesus.

April 11th 2017

488 A family returned to tell me that their baby daughter was still fit and well after a prayer six months ago. Their baby was in a cast. After prayer the cast was removed two months quicker to what the hospital had instructed. All complications and problems that the doctors said could have happened, didn't happen. They reported that she is walking around and very happy. Thank you Jesus.

May 9th 2017

489 Leaving the healing meeting at Victory Gospel Church, a lady was outside begging. Asked her if she had any pain. She said yes. She had pain in her shoulder and also down her back. Allowed me to pray for her. God's presence came, healed her shoulder and took away her pain. Her back was also healed by the Holy Spirit even though my hand was on her shoulder. She felt two discs move in her back. At the time she was overwhelmed with the presence of God. She said that she believes in Jesus and prays.

May 12th 2017

490 Met a young woman in town. She had a drug addiction and was a prostitute. She had scarring all up her arms and was in considerable pain. Pain in her hands and womb. The fire of the Holy Spirit touched her, and all pain left her body

491 Beggar outside burger king with crutches. Word of knowledge concerning his knee. He was covered in sleeping bags, so I wasn't sure if his problem was with his knee but by faith I went over and asked him if he had a problem with his knee. He explained that he was sleeping rough, there were some used heroin needles on the floor that he did not see, when he laid down to sleep, one of the needles went into the back of his knee. He had to go to hospital. At one point he thought that he was going to lose his leg. The leg was still painful and still. Prayed with him and the healing power came. I believe that he will be 100% restored. Thank you Jesus.

492 Working in a seaside town, got talking to a man called Rob in his sixties from Glasgow. He told me that his wife had passed away three years ago and that he had a breakdown. Previous to that he was a boxer. Scottish champion. Was then able to ask him if I could pray for him. Prayed for healing to a broken heart. Then my phone rang, and it was my friend who was also a Scottish boxer! I passed my phone over to Rob, they both used to go to the same boxing club in Glasgow! Thank you God for the fruitfulness of your glory. Love never fails.

493 Visiting my son Peter for the afternoon, we decided to go to a car boot sale at Walton on Thames. A lady walked past me, and the Lord spoke to me as she had a support on her wrist and around her thumb. I asked her what the problem was, she said that she had been in pain with it for one and a half years. I asked to pray, and she said yes. Instructed by the Holy Spirit, I rubbed her thumb as I believe it was a tendon problem even though she didn't tell me what was wrong. I believe God reconditioned that area and healed the tendons. Instant healing and all pain left. She took off the support and I said to her that she would never need the support again as God has healed you.

494 Prior to that, I was in Bournemouth, there was a young lady sitting on the floor, she had her family around her. The Lord gave me a word for her that she was going to become a doctor and she was not to give up her training as it would be hard at times but worth it at the end. She would become a doctor in many countries. She then told me that her dream was to build a hospital! Praise God.

September 15th 2017

495 I was sitting in my front garden reading some testimonies when a man walked past. He was talking to himself saying, "My legs are xxxxxx." On hearing this, I jumped up and then asked him what he had just said. He then repeated what he said; then informing me his legs had been in pain for six months. I asked if I could pray for him. He said yes. I then laid my hands onto his legs. Off he went. Robert then returned a few days later to confirm that all pain had left, and he thought it was crazy that I just appeared from nowhere! Amen.

November 11th 2017

496 I was able to minister to a Kenyan lady a few days ago, she had a serious problem with cysts. She was due to have surgery to remove them. I prayed for her. Yesterday, I got a phone call from her to say that when she went for her operation, the doctors had to apologise as they could not find any cysts. They said that due to the nature of these cysts, it was medically impossible for this to happen. Apparently the doctor seemed to be in a state of shock. Praise God.

January 13th 2018

497 A man named Wayne returned to tell me that after prayer, his toes have uncurled and the cyst in his knee has disappeared. He should have had surgery to remove this, but it was not needed.

February 7th 2018

498 In Malta, met a lady called Zinnia and her daughter whilst having dinner in the hotel restaurant. I noticed that she had a broken thumb. She said that it was broken off from the base since November and was quite painful, especially in the cold weather. I asked if I could pray for her. She said yes. I placed my hand on hers and prayed to Jesus to knit the bone back together. Her hand got really hot. She took off her support and had full movement restored. Complete healing. She also came back to report that her stomach pain had left, and her stomach had gone down since prayer.

February 14th 2018

499 Received a testimony from a lady that was healed from depression and fear. She was horribly abused and suffered with this for years. She said that her mind is now free, and she has clarity. Thank you Lord, I give you all the glory, honour and praise.

500 *After re-reading this journal of healings and testimonies, I pray that this will teach people to receive their healing and believe to receive. There is a great power of testimonies and by the stripes we are healed. Jesus has paid the price. The blood of Jesus has overcome the works of the devil 100%. Healing is our portion. God has done this and wants to do it again. Praise God. Thank you Lord Jesus. Amen.*

They triumphed over him by the blood of the Lamb and by the word of their testimony.

Revelation 12:11 NIV

CONTACT THE AUTHOR

IAN KRUGER
(aka "The Happy Hotdog Man")

Ian resides in Southampton in the United Kingdom and is willing to share his experience and testimony with as many as are willing to hear.

If you wish to contact Ian or invite him to minister at your church or conference, please email him below.

iankrugerelisha1963@hotmail.com

SUPPORT THE AUTHOR

Ian believes that God is now calling him into a teaching, and impartation healing ministry so the Body of Christ can also do these works for God's kingdom in their everyday life.

Ian would also like to write two more books.

His request is for financial support as it takes finances to travel etc. so he can fulfil the work of the ministry.

To those who are looking to sponsor and support a fruitful work of God, they would be giving into a proven ministry over twelve years which Ian believes God now wants him to share with the Body of Christ.

Please consider sponsoring and supporting this ministry and to do so, simply contact Ian through his email. *iankrugerelisha1963@hotmail.com*

Thank you.

To God be the glory, honour and praise.

Amen.

Printed in Poland
by Amazon Fulfillment
Poland Sp. z o.o., Wrocław

54618836R00125